Beautiful Easy Gardens

Beautiful Easy Gardens

A WEEK-BY-WEEK GUIDE
TO **PLANTING, HARVESTING,**
AND **ENJOYING**
TEN GREAT GARDENS

by Laurence Sombke
The Environmental Gardener

The Globe Pequot Press
Old Saybrook, Connecticut

Text illustrations by Joy Stampes
Book design by Nancy Freeborn

Library of Congress Cataloging-in-Publication Data

Sombke, Laurence.
    Beautiful easy gardens : a week-by-week guide to planting, harvesting, and enjoying ten great gardens / Laurence Sombke. — 1st ed.
        p. cm.
    ISBN 1-56440-215-0   ISBN 1-56440-167-7
    1. Organic gardening. 2. Low maintenance gardening. 3. Gardens—Designs and plans. I. Title.
    SB453.5.S66 1993
    635'.0484—dc20   92-39581
                                                    CIP

Manufactured in the United States of America
First Edition/First Printing

DEDICATION

I want to dedicate this book to my wife, Catherine Herman, who always seems to know what's best for me, even when I don't, and who allowed me to feature her own backyard creation for this book's Shady Glen chapter.

Contents

Acknowledgments

I want to acknowledge the dedication, hard work, help, and inspiration of many people for the creation of this book: my agent Denise Marcil and my editor Laura Strom; my mother- and father-in-law, Betty and Frank Herman, who have let me experiment with all my gardening ideas on their property; my parents, for getting me started in gardening; our friend Phyllis Luntta, who helped us pay the bills; and my kids, Henry and Kit, who like to help Daddy in the garden.

Introduction

Welcome to my garden, and thanks for buying this book. I think you are going to like *Beautiful Easy Gardens* because it features the kinds of gardens that you and thousands of other people just like you have told me you want.

I speak several times each year at flower shows, horticultural societies, and botanical gardens and on radio and television talk shows. I've learned that people want three things in a garden:

1. To grow vegetables, fruits, herbs, and flowers that have not been sprayed with chemical pesticides.
2. To easily maintain the garden without spending a lot of time and effort.
3. To enhance the beauty of the home landscape, adding some special style or uniqueness.

I have done my best to respond to your requests in these ten garden plans. I made them small; none are greater than 10 feet by 15 feet except the Cottage Orchard and the Cook's Salad Garden. I've stripped out sweaty garden tasks such as hoeing and dragging sprinklers and hoses all over the place. I've shown you what to add to the soil and how to use mulch so your garden won't wilt under the hot summer sun.

You are going to create gardens that are so strong and healthy that you won't need to use any synthetic chemical pesticides or fertilizers. Instead you will sparingly use natural, organic pest controls and fertilizers. You will use less water and have a better looking garden with the watering system I have recommended.

Eight of the gardens in this book will grow food for your family and friends. I've included over fifty recipes, which I hope will help you enjoy what you have grown. The other two gardens are flower beds; both are colorful and foolproof.

All of the gardens in this book are set up on a weekly and seasonal time schedule. I give you something to do in the garden every week from early spring till late fall. Each weekly activity is really a "work window," meaning

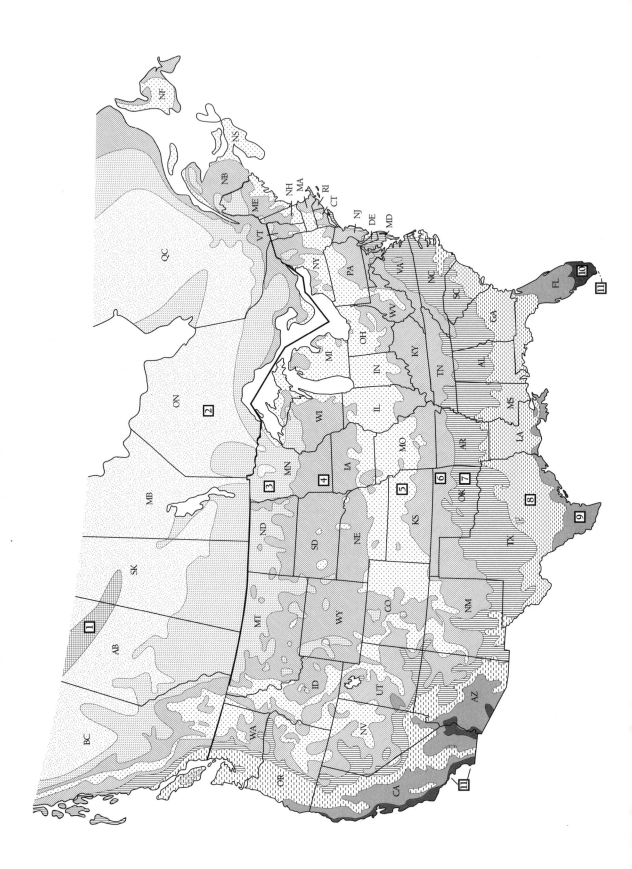

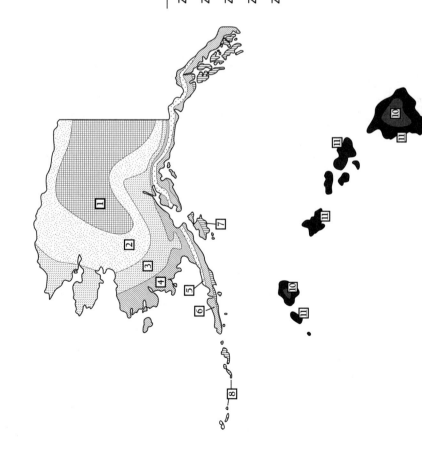

RANGE OF ANNUAL MINIMUM TEMPERATURES FOR EACH ZONE

ZONE 1   Below 50° F
ZONE 2   -50° to -40° F
ZONE 3   -40° to -30° F
ZONE 4   -30° to -20° F
ZONE 5   -20° to -10° F

ZONE 6   -10° to 0° F
ZONE 7   0° to 10° F
ZONE 8   10° to 20° F
ZONE 9   20° to 30° F
ZONE 10   30° to 40° F

ZONE 11   Above 40° F

that you have a couple of weeks to get the chores completed. Because there are varying climates and the seasons come and go at slightly different times in different regions, each weekly work window is two to three weeks long. For instance, if you live in Springfield, Illinois, you can start your garden two to three weeks earlier than if you live in Albany, New York, but you are both doing the same work at approximately the same time.

Please take a look at the United States Department of Agriculture (USDA) hardiness zone map on the previous pages. This map tells you when you can expect the last frost in spring and the first frost in autumn to occur. This is what I mean about varying climates in different parts of the United States. Find your location on the map and learn when your first and last frost-free dates are likely to occur. Of course, even within these zones there will be variations caused by elevation, proximity to bodies of water, and other geographical influences. Ask your neighbors when they start planting things outdoors and consider weighing their experience when you make out your personal planting schedule.

Be flexible. Cut yourself a little slack. You don't need to be a slave to these work windows and you don't need to plant every little thing I tell you to plant. Plant something different if you want, but do try to follow the weekly schedule at least in a general way.

It is very important that you read the first three chapters in the book on tools, getting started, and environmental pest control. You will then have a background of general garden knowledge, and you will be familiar with the terms and techniques used in the following chapters. Almost all of the information in the first three chapters will be repeated or mentioned in the individual chapters as the gardening calendar progresses. But the more familiar you are with things such as fertilizers, mulch, soaker hoses, forked spades, codling moth traps, and dormant oil spray, the less likely you will be to get confused when the time comes to use them.

Once you have decided which gardens you are going to plant, I strongly advise you to read through the entire Weekly Guide or Seasonal Guide early in the season, before you start your project. This way you will know what to expect, how to prepare for it, and how to manage your personal schedule so you can get certain critical projects done when you have the time. It will also give you a feel for the seasonal rhythm of the garden, allowing you to look forward to a wonderful year working in and enjoying your beautiful, easy garden.

PART ONE

Gardening Fundamentals

A Gardener's Tools and Equipment

The average amateur gardener needs a few well-selected tools to get the job done right. The right tools will make your task a lot easier, giving you more time to enjoy the fruits of your labor. There is a tremendous variation in price and quality of tools and an endless selection of gadgets, some good and some not so good. In this chapter I will tell you which tools you should buy and which tools you should rent or borrow.

The first rule is to buy the best-quality tool you can afford. I have had enough garden tools bend and break right in my hands to know it is not worth it to buy cheap ones. You don't have to be extravagant, but you should spend a little more to buy one high-quality spade, for instance, instead of several cheaper ones. Buy a tool that you expect to last you for the rest of your life. I use forty-year-old garden tools that have been passed down from my wife's grandfather.

There are several good places to buy tools. At your local hardware store, garden center, or home center, you can actually get your hands on the tools and feel their quality. Mail-order catalogs are great, too, because they offer a larger selection of quality tools, many of them imported, and usually include detailed descriptions of the different tools. I've included a list of catalogs at the end of this chapter. Finally, be sure to check out yard sales and tag sales for garden tools. Some people just don't know what they are getting rid of, and you can often find excellent-quality used tools at rock-bottom prices. You may even find a few valuable antique tools.

The second rule when it comes to tools is to take good care of them. Brush dirt and moisture off metal tools and wipe them with an oily rag before you put them away. Wipe the wooden handles with mineral oil or vegetable oil once in a while to protect the wood. Change the oil every year on power tools and keep them clean and dry. Take care of your tools, and they will take care of you.

Tools for the gardener can be roughly divided into six categories: digging tools, hand tools, planting tools, watering tools, composting tools, and power tools. I am not going to list all the different types of tools you *could* have. Instead I will give you a short list of tools that you will actually need to use.

The gardens in this book are designed to be small and to require little maintenance, which means you won't need the array of tools that gardeners with large plots must have. For instance, I don't suggest you buy a common garden hoe. Rather than ask you to stand out in the hot sun chopping weeds with a hoe every week, I suggest mulching the garden heavily once so that later you can sit back and enjoy a glass of iced tea.

Digging Tools

Forked Spade. Also known as a digging fork, a spading fork, or a garden fork, this is the most versatile garden tool you can own. You can use it to dig up the soil and prepare the beds for most of the gardens described in this book. It is also good as a compost fork and can be used to dig holes for transplanting. Look for a tool with a forged head made of heavy-gauge stainless or carbon steel firmly attached to a hardwood or steel shaft that is topped with a D-shaped steel handle. The tool should be about waist high.

Level-Head Garden Rake. You will need a heavy, steel garden rake to smooth the soil and rake out the rocks, roots, and debris before you plant. Don't confuse this with a lawn rake, which has long flexible teeth to rake up leaves and grass clippings. Choose a rake that has a forged, one-piece steel head with curved teeth attached to a sturdy hardwood shaft.

Edger. An edger is a steel semicircle attached to a waist-high shaft that you use to dig narrow trenches or edges around your flower or vegetable garden to separate it from the lawn. It really does give your gardens a tidy, neat look. Look for a good-quality edger with a slight lip on the top side so that when you press down on it with your foot, you won't dig into your shoe.

Hand Tools

Trowel. A trowel is indispensable for transplanting flower and vegetable bedding plants into your garden. You can also use it to shovel and smooth out a small area, or to dig holes to plant tulip and daffodil bulbs. I use both wide-blade and narrow-blade trowels—it's a toss-up which type I use more often. Choose the kind that feels comfortable in your hand, or just splurge and get both. Look for a solid forged, heavy-duty steel trowel that won't bend when you use it.

Pruning Shears. Also known as hand pruners, or secateurs, pruning shears will be useful to you when you start planting roses, shrubs, vines, and small trees. You can also use pruning shears to cut roses and other flowers for bouquets and to cut perennials back in the fall. There are pruning shears for big jobs, small jobs, left- and right-handed persons, and more. You won't need anything more than lightweight pruning shears. Choose a pair that feels good in your hands and has brightly colored handles so that you won't lose them in the garden.

Lopping Shears. Lopping shears are long-handled pruning shears designed to handle larger shrubs and bushes with branches up to $1^1/_2$ inches thick. You won't need these right away, but eventually you will if you do any landscaping in your yard. Look for steel blades and sturdy handles.

Pruning Saw. You will need a pruning saw only if you plant the Cottage Orchard Garden described in this book, and then only when the trees are a mature 8 to 10 feet tall and the branches are more than 2 inches thick. Buy a curved-bladed saw, with a wooden handle, that cuts on the pull action or draw stroke rather than on the push stroke.

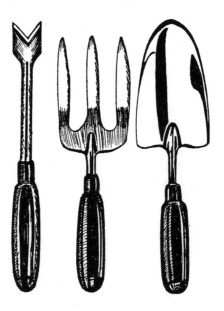

Planting Tools

Planting Line. You can easily make this tool out of two 12-inch pointed stakes and 20 feet of nylon or cotton string. Ready-made ones are available in stores and through catalogs. A planting line enables you to plant straight rows in the garden. You simply put one stake in the ground, run the cord along the planting bed, and then poke the other stake in the ground at the other end. It really does help.

Seed-Starting Kit. Also known as propagators, some companies now offer fully stocked seed-planting kits, which are very convenient. It is a lot of fun to start your own tomato or flower plants from seed indoors, and you get a chance to enjoy a wider variety of seed selections. The kits come complete with a tabletop-sized greenhouse, planting pots, soil mixture, and a watering tray.

Plant Label Stakes. I can't tell you how often I have heard a frustrated gardener complain, "I planted something there, and now I can't remember what it is." Well, don't let this happen to you. Buy plant label stakes, made of either plastic, wood, or metal; write the names of your plants on them, preferably with a waterproof marker; then place them in the ground nearby. Most of the major botanical gardens do this—why shouldn't you?

Watering Tools

The tools in this section are selected with water conservation in mind. Almost everywhere there is some water shortage at one time or another, and gardeners should be in the forefront of wise water use.

Watering Can. Watering cans are convenient for watering bedding plants when you first transplant them into the ground and then again every few days until they get established. Watering cans come in various sizes, shapes, and colors, so pick one you like the best. I prefer a galvanized-steel can with a standard, not elongated, spout. Heavy-duty plastic cans are also quite good. I think a 2-gallon can full of water is about as heavy as the average person can handle.

Rubber Hose and Nozzle. Don't buy cheap plastic hoses. They tend to kink, crack, and become useless in a very short time. Buy a 50-foot length of reinforced rubber hose with heavy-duty brass couplings. You will need your rubber hose to water trees and to hook up to your soaker hose. I suggest you buy a standard-size solid polished-brass nozzle, which gives you a variable stream of water from a light sprinkle to a hard stream. A good quality hose and nozzle can handle any amount of pressure and will never break.

Soaker Hose. Soaker hoses ooze water out through the pores of the rubber hose itself. With a soaker hose you will conserve up to 70 percent of the water you used to waste when you watered your garden with a sprinkler. Furthermore, a soaker hose does a better job because the water can slowly seep deep down into the soil, where it can be stored and used as the plants need it.

Rain Barrel. The old-fashioned rain barrel is rapidly making a solid comeback. You can collect hundreds of gallons of precious rainwater during an average shower. Simply position the barrel at the end of your downspout and collect the water as it runs through your gutter system. Rain barrels are usually made of heavy-gauge plastic, but an attractive wooden barrel would look nice in your yard and garden.

Composting Tools

A typical family can compost up to 25 percent of their yard and kitchen waste. Compost is the best source of organic matter for your garden. A few simple tools are all it takes.

Compost Bin. Practical, yard-sized compost bins are now widely available in catalogs and wherever garden products are sold. There are compost bins made of cedar, pine, redwood, heavy-duty plastic, or vinyl-coated wire fencing. Your choice will be based on aesthetics, because all of them work equally well.

Compost Fork. A compost fork, or turning tool, is important in making compost. You have to turn or stir compost to aerate it so that all the materials in the bin will decompose. I use my forked spade to turn compost, which works quite well. But I suggest you invest in a compost turner, a short rod with propellerlike blades on the end, which takes much of the back-breaking labor out of compost making.

Power Tools

Rear-Tined Tiller (Rotary Tiller). Having your garden tilled with a power tiller is an important part of a low-maintenance garden program. Of course, you can dig the garden up by hand from day one, but that can be a lot of work. You will be able to dig up your garden after a couple of years of adding organic matter so that the soil becomes loose and friable, but early on I suggest you have it tilled. Tillers are expensive. If you feel you can afford one, by all means buy one. I have one and I love it. But think about renting a tiller for a day or hiring a lawn company to come around to till your garden for you. Look in the Yellow Pages or in the classified section of your newspaper.

The Best of the Rest

Garden Cart or Wheelbarrow. I strongly suggest you invest in a two-wheeled garden cart or in a wheelbarrow. You can use either one to haul compost, organic matter, leaves, grass, fertilizer, bedding plants, mulch, watering cans, and tools.

Carryall. By a carryall I mean some sort of basket in which you can store and carry your hand tools, seeds, plant-marking stakes, and other little odds and ends. A wooden Sussex basket is quite nice, but so is a mason's or painter's canvas bag or even a hard plastic shopping basket.

Bushel Basket. A bushel basket is handy for filling up with weeds and other yard and garden debris. It is also good for harvesting corn, melons, lettuce, beans, apples, or whatever you are growing.

Gloves. Unless you don't care if your hands are bruised, blistered, rough, raw, and sorely in need of Bag Balm, you should buy and wear a pair of gardening gloves, at least until your skin toughens up. Inexpensive, washable cotton gloves are flexible and suitable. Leather gloves are much longer lasting, but they are a bit stiffer.

Pocket Knife. I never go out to the garden without a pocket knife. I use either my Swiss Army knife or a carbon-steel, wooden-handled folding knife

I bought at a hardware store in Marseilles. A pocket knife is handy for harvesting lettuce and arugula, picking flowers, cutting string, and for a million other little things, including slicing open that first melon or tomato fresh from the vine.

<hr />

Here's a list of mail-order catalogs that carry all or most of the tools listed above, plus a lot of wonderful tools and accessories you may feel are just as important.

A. M. Leonard, Inc., 6665 Spiker Road, Piqua, OH 45356; (800) 543–8955. Purveyors of tools and supplies to professional gardeners and landscapers. Eighty-page catalog full of great buys.

Gardener's Supply, 128 Intervale Road, Burlington, VT 05401; (802) 863–1700. Large selection of tools, irrigation equipment, cooking supplies, and other products.

Harmony Farm Supply, P.O. Box 460, Grafton, CA 95444; (707) 823–9125. Extensive selection of irrigation equipment and comprehensive collection of hand and power tools.

Kinsman Company, River Road, Point Pleasant, PA 18950; (215) 297–5613. Very good selection of English and American-made shovels, rakes, hand tools, and watering cans.

Langenbach, P.O. Box 453, Blairstown, NJ 07825; (800) 362–1991. Quality selection of tools, irrigation equipment, shears, and some power tools.

The Natural Gardening Company, 217 San Anselmo Avenue, San Anselmo, CA 94960; (415) 456–5060. Choice selection of good quality tools as well as seeds and other supplies.

Smith & Hawken, 25 Corte Madera, Mill Valley, CA 94941; (415) 383–2000. Classy garden tools, furniture, and clothing.

Walter Nicke Co., 36 McLeod Lane, Topsfield, MA 01983; (508) 887–3388. Catalog lists more than 300 tools, including a good selection of shears and clippers.

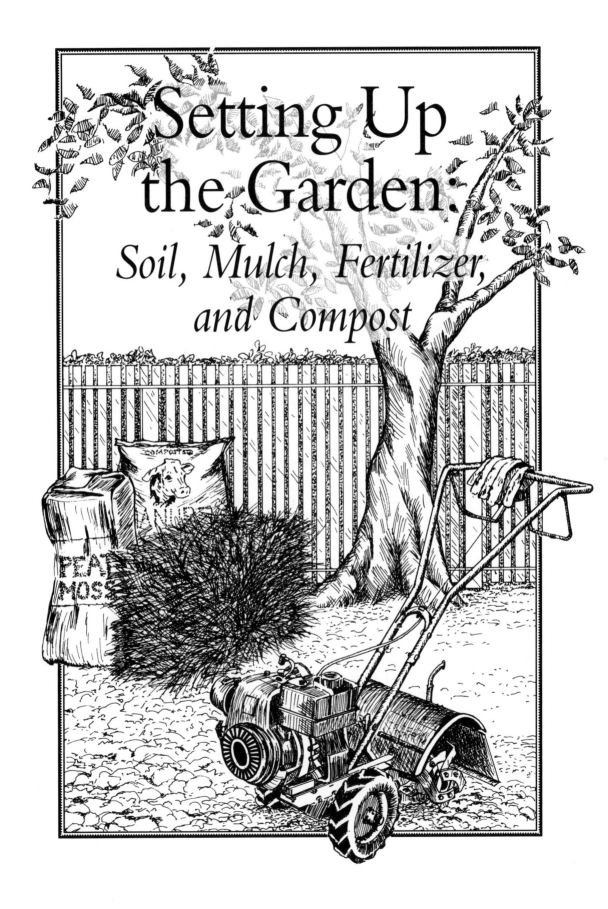

Setting Up the Garden:
Soil, Mulch, Fertilizer, and Compost

How to get your garden off to a good start is the most important information in this book. How well you prepare the soil and how you manage the garden will determine how beautiful your flowers are, how productive your herbs and vegetables are, and how well your garden can withstand the ravages of insects, diseases, and drought.

When I give presentations at botanical gardens and flower shows and when I listen to garden call-in shows, I hear many of the same problems from people: "My flowers wilt during the day no matter how much I water them," or "My tomato plants always seem to turn yellow." The advice usually given on radio and television shows is to spray with some kind of chemical.

Although chemicals might have a place in some gardens, the "spray first" philosophy does not go to the root of the problem. Pests and diseases are symptoms of a garden that is not being managed properly.

Tending a garden is in some ways very much like taking care of your own health. If you eat a well-balanced diet, get plenty of sleep, exercise regularly, avoid stress, and moderate your alcohol intake, you will most likely be a healthy person. Your body has a way of fighting off diseases all by itself. If you party all night, eat junk food, and slump in front of the television every night, you will eventually get sick.

The same holds true for your garden. You can't treat your soil like dirt. If you neglect the soil, spray it with too many chemicals, or douse it with the wrong kind of fertilizer, your garden will eventually suffer from drought and attack by pests. But if you dig the soil well, give it lots of sunshine and water, and add plenty of organic matter and the right amount of fertilizer, your garden will be able to withstand drought and fight off most pests and diseases all by itself.

In this chapter I am going to tell you how to find the right location for your garden, how to dig and prepare the soil, how to enrich and fertilize the soil, how to apply mulch, how to water you garden, and how to make compost.

It's true that it takes a little more work and a little more time to start your garden off the right way. You are going to be working with nature, not against it. Although nature takes a little more time to work than chemicals do, I think it's worth it. Let's get started.

Finding the Right Place for Your Garden

Finding the right place to put your garden depends a lot on what type of property you have and how your yard is laid out. The real key to any successful garden is that it must get at least six hours of direct sunshine each day.

If you have a shady yard and you are not in the mood to cut down all your trees, be happy. You can plant and grow a beautiful shade garden. Just turn to the chapter in this book and plant "A Shady Glen." I have a shady backyard that we've planted as a shady woodland garden, and all summer long we appreciate the cool shade both inside the house and in the yard itself.

But if you want to grow fruits, vegetables, and flowers, you must have sunshine. If you are a little short on sunshine, you may consider pruning back a few tree limbs or shrubs or even removing a tree and replanting a new tree in a different part of the yard. Think of it as rearranging your furniture or redecorating your house.

None of the gardens in this book, except A Cottage Orchard and A Cook's Salad Garden, are larger than 10 feet wide and 15 feet long. You of course can expand your gardens in any way you see fit, but I have deliberately kept them small to enable you to take care of them with less than two hours of work most weeks.

Find an area in your yard that measures 10 by 15 feet and mark it out with stakes. Make sure the area is well drained, which means that it doesn't remain soggy after a heavy rain. Remove and discard any debris, sticks, and stones. If the area is part of your lawn, remove the sod and replant it in parts of your lawn that need it, or just get rid of it.

Digging and Preparing the Soil

Rototill your garden—either have it done for you or dig the garden up yourself by hand. Be sure the soil is turned down to a depth of at least 6 inches.

Carefully remove any plant roots or stems you find in the soil. If you don't, these same weeds will resprout, and you will have a garden full of weeds in no time. Also remove as many rocks as possible from the garden.

Now is the time to have a soil test done on your soil. A soil test is no more complicated that an early pregnancy test. You can do it yourself with an inexpensive kit purchased from your local lawn and garden center or cooperative extension office.

A soil test determines the chemical balance, called pH, of your soil. The pH scale rates the soil from 1 to 10, with acid soils measuring from 1 to 6 and alkaline soils 7 to 10. Most plants prefer to grow in soil with a neutral pH balance of 6.0 to 7.0. If your test registers below 6.0, which is common in New England, the Northeast, and many parts of the South, you will need to add lime to return it to neutral. If it shows a reading above 7.0, which is not very common at all, you can correct that imbalance by adding compost to the soil.

Commonly your soil test will show a pH level of 5.0 or slightly lower. To raise that back to the 6.0 to 7.0 range, simply add 8 to 10 pounds (approximately 9 to 10 cups) of ground, powdered limestone, which you can buy at your garden center. This is enough for the 150-square-foot gardens in this book. Just sprinkle it over the soil and dig it in with the organic matter and fertilizer.

It's a good idea, although not absolutely necessary, to take a soil test every year. You will probably need to add limestone to a slightly acidic soil every other year or every three years, although recent studies have shown that an annual application of 2 to 4 inches of compost will balance a soil without the addition of any minerals.

Enriching and Fertilizing the Soil

Add a 2- to 4-inch layer of organic matter over the entire surface of the garden plot. The best organic matter is homemade or store-bought compost, rotted hay or manure from a farmer's barn, shredded leaves, composted manure, Canadian sphagnum peat moss, or peat humus. Most of the gardens in this book are 150 to 200 square feet in size. You will need four to six bushels of compost or composted manure, two to three 4-cubic-foot bags of sphagnum peat moss or four to five 40-pound bags of store-bought compost. Simply open the bags and spread the organic matter around the garden.

Now that the garden is limed, if necessary, and the organic matter spread on top, you need to add the natural organic fertilizer. If you have a country garden, you might be able to get livestock manure as your primary source of fertilizer, but if you garden in town, I suggest you buy a bag of natural organic fertilizer from a commercial company—Ringer, EarthGro, Koos, Espoma, Vermont Fertilizer Co., Nature Safe, Gardener's Best, or others.

Chemical fertilizers are made of natural gas, whereas natural organic fertilizers are made of bone meal, compost, wheat germ, sunflower seed hulls, dairy whey, and other byproducts of agriculture or food-processing industries. I prefer natural organic fertilizers because they feed the garden slowly over a long period of time, just the way nature does. They also contribute organic matter to the soil.

Fertilizer bears numbers such as 5-5-5 or 8-6-4 on the label. These numbers stand for the percentage of nitrogen, phosphorus, and potassium, or N-P-K, in the fertilizer. These are the essential nutrients that all gardens need, and these three numbers will vary from brand to brand. To fertilize your garden all summer long, you will need to use from $2^{1}/_{2}$ to 5 pounds of natural organic fertilizer. If a 10-pound bag of fertilizer is the only size available, buy it and don't worry. It will store safely in a cool, dry place until you use it up over several years. Follow the package instructions and apply the recommended amount of fertilizer now.

Rototill or dig up the garden again to incorporate all the organic matter and fertilizer into the top 4 to 6 inches of soil. Rake the garden smooth.

At this point it's a good idea to add a pound of worms to the soil. Worms are a garden's best friend. They aerate the soil and make it more crumbly by tunneling through it, and they leave their own fertilizer behind as they go. Any kind of worms that you can buy at a garden center or at your local bait shop is fine for your garden.

Mulching the Garden

Mulch is a blanket of organic or inorganic material applied on the surface of your garden and around the plants. It keeps weeds under control because it smothers them, and it helps keep the garden moist by preventing water from evaporating out of the soil.

I do not recommend using black plastic, paper, or fabric mulches, mainly for aesthetic reasons. I just don't like the way they look. Other people like them and use them successfully, and if you want to, be my guest.

For vegetable gardens I prefer natural organic mulches such as straw, old hay, shredded leaves, dried grass clippings, and compost. (Avoid fresh hay and grass clippings from lawns that have gone to seed. Both contain seeds that might sprout and create more weeds.) In addition to retaining water and stifling weeds, mulch will decompose and add additional organic matter to your garden, making the soil more crumbly, rich, and water conserving.

For flowers I prefer a blend of peat moss and/or compost and shredded pine bark, pine needles, or wood chips. You will need at least six bags of shredded bark or pine needles and one to two bags of peat moss to mulch the flower beds described in this book and six bales of straw or hay to mulch the vegetable gardens.

Keeping the Garden Watered

A garden will die without water. Your job is to make the best use of the limited water resources we are all facing now. You are already off to a good start because by adding organic matter and fertilizer to the garden, your soil will act as a sponge or reservoir to capture and hold water whether it comes from the sky or the hose. Also, deeply tilled enriched soil will encourage your plants' roots to burrow deep into the soil, making them more adept at getting water and making them stronger and more drought resistant. By applying mulch you have also helped retain what water does reach your garden.

There still may come times, however, when watering is necessary. Here are two rules of wise watering: (1) Apply water as close to the root zone as possible, and (2) Water slowly and infrequently.

Spraying your garden with a quick shower every night is wasting water and ruining your garden. Plants absorb water through their root systems, which are buried deep in the soil. Spraying the leaves of the plants from above is worthless and can actually damage the plants. Roots will go wherever the water is. If you give your garden a quick spritz of water that penetrates only the top inch of soil, that's where the roots will go, making your plants weak and susceptible to drought.

The best way to water your garden is with a soaker hose or drip hose that is laid on top of the soil and then covered with mulch. Soaker hoses release their water very slowly; they actually "sweat out" the water through the walls of the hose itself. Drip hoses release their water slowly through tiny holes in the hose. Slow watering allows the soil to absorb more water and store it 6 to 8 inches underground. The plants then draw on the water as needed.

Soaker hoses soak the ground to a width of 18 inches on either side of the hose itself. Buy one 50-foot length of soaker hose and snake it or loop it through the garden in an S pattern. If you expand your garden, you can easily add another length of soaker hose.

You don't want to run a soaker hose from the spigot on your house out to the garden. Instead, leave your soaker hose in place in the garden and attach a high-quality rubber or reinforced plastic hose between the garden and the house whenever you want to water.

Water your garden no more than once a week for two to four hours. That's how long it takes to soak the ground to a depth of 6 inches. If you are getting an inch of rainfall every week, you won't need to water the garden at all. It is important to refrain from watering the garden too early in the season to help train the roots to dig down deep in the soil.

Since you are going to water with a soaker hose, it doesn't really matter what time of day you water the garden. If you have a choice, water in the early morning, up till noon, or in the late afternoon or early evening.

Making Compost

Compost is the most beneficial ingredient you can add to your garden. It is rich in organic matter and beneficial microorganisms, and it contains some nutrients. If your town or city has a municipal composting program and they allow you to come out to the composting site and take what you need, by all means get some bushel baskets and go out there. Your garden will really thrive from annual applications of compost.

Making compost is as simple as following a recipe or putting together a model airplane. All you are trying to do is assist nature to decompose grass clippings, leaves, hedge trimmings, kitchen scraps, and dead plants into a soil-like substance called humus. Just follow these simple steps:

1. Buy a compost bin that will look attractive in your backyard so that your neighbors won't complain about it. I prefer the bins made out of heavy-duty recycled plastic, but I also own bins made of cedar slats and fencing wire.

2. Place the bin in a semishaded area that is near enough to the house or garden so that it is easy to put things into it.

3. Add a blend of ingredients to your compost: high-nitrogen ingredients, like grass clippings or kitchen scraps, and high-carbon ingredients, like shredded leaves and hedge trimmings.

4. If your compost dries out, add 2 to 5 gallons of water. If it is too wet, let it dry out.

5. Turn or stir the compost pile once a month. This incorporates all the ingredients and helps things decompose faster.

6. Add a cupful or handful of compost activator to the pile whenever you turn it. Activator helps give the pile a little kick start to get it moving along faster.

7. Be patient. It takes at least two to four months to make compost, longer if you keep adding kitchen scraps to the pile as I do.

8. Do not add dog, cat, or human feces to the pile. Do not add meat, bones, cheese, cooking oil, eggs, or mollusk shells to the pile. They take too long to decompose and they attract critters.

Compost is done when it looks more like a crumbly, rich soil than like last week's peanut-butter sandwich. Simply spread the compost out on the garden or under the bushes and start making more.

Look, your garden loves compost, and if you don't make it yourself, you are going to have to buy it. You have to get rid of that yard waste and kitchen waste anyway. Sending it to the landfill is not environmentally beneficial, so you might as well make compost.

It is hoped that you will refer back to this chapter often. In summary, I can't stress enough the importance of these guidelines: dig the soil deep; enrich the soil with large doses of organic matter every year; always use an organic, degradable mulch to stifle weeds; conserve water; and make your own compost. These procedures are all good for the environment and even better for your garden.

Environmental
Pest Control

*Y*ou would be hard-pressed to find producers of synthetic chemical insecticides, fungicides, and herbicides who would tell you that their products are not safe and effective if used carefully. It certainly is your right to believe them and use whatever pesticides you feel are necessary. For my part, however, I am not convinced that synthetic chemical pesticides are completely safe for me, my family, and the environment. There are mounting reports that pesticides are reaching into our drinking water and are harmful to wildlife.

The most important thing for you to know as a small-scale gardener is that you do not have to use pesticides if you do not want to. You can have a beautiful garden that is easy to maintain without the use of pesticides. That is not to say that diseases, insects, weeds, and critters are not going to do their best to destroy your garden. They will, but I'm going to show you how to outsmart these pests and control them in a safe, sane, environmental manner without causing you extra work.

In this chapter I will give you my Ten-Point Environmental Pest-Control Program, followed by a brief description of cultural, mechanical, biological, and botanical pest-control products, and then a concise list of fruits, vegetables, and flowers along with their common pests and courses of action to control them. All the information in this chapter will be incorporated later into the individual chapters, but it is important to read this chapter first for a good background knowledge of environmental pest control.

Ten-Point Environmental Pest-Control Program

1. *Stop using chemicals.* You don't need chemicals. If you have been using them in the past, just say no. Go cold turkey. Chemicals tend to kill not only the pest you are after but also all the insects and birds that are beneficial to your

garden. Give your garden a chance to be vigorous and strong without the use of chemicals.

Note: Most garden chemicals are considered highly toxic hazardous waste. *Do not dispose of them yourself.* Take them to a household hazardous-waste collection center or call your sanitation, solid waste, or public works department for disposal advice in your area.

2. *Build the soil.* Following the advice about soil preparation in the previous chapter, you need to add organic matter and natural organic fertilizer to your garden each year. This will help make your garden so fertile that your plants will grow so vigorous and healthy that they will be better able to withstand any pest attack.

3. *Water correctly.* Both overwatering and underwatering can provide a breeding ground for diseases that will kill your plants. Drought-stricken plants are a perfect target for pests. A well-tilled soil enriched with organic matter conserves water and keeps plants stronger during drought.

4. *Attract birds to your backyard.* Birds eat enormous numbers of insects. Make them feel at home by providing bird baths and trees and bushes for them to nest in. Other good animals and insects you want nearby are bats, garden snakes, toads, ladybugs, mantises, and certain types of wasps. A chemical-free garden and yard is a good habitat for all of these animals.

5. *Plant disease-resistant varieties.* Certain varieties of plants are more immune to diseases than are others. Scientists and plant breeders have continued to improve our selection of these plants. Natural disease resistance will be a primary reason for selecting the types of plants recommended in this book.

6. *Move your plants around.* This is called crop rotation in agriculture. It simply means planting lettuce, for example, in a different part of the garden each year to confuse insects and diseases and make it more difficult for them to do their damage. Of course, this isn't practical with trees or perennials, but it is highly advisable with all other plants in the garden.

7. *Control weeds with mulch.* Every square foot of garden soil has hundreds of weed seeds just waiting to sprout. The best way to control these weeds is to simply smother them with mulch such as straw, hay, shredded leaves, or compost. Besides stifling weeds without chemicals, you are adding organic matter back to the soil as the mulch decomposes.

8. *Know thine enemy.* Chemical pest control relies on a "spray first and ask questions later" approach. The environmental approach means identifying the specific pest that is causing problems and then treating it accordingly.

9. *Try the least toxic remedy first.* Certain bugs, such as aphids, can be cured by spraying them with water or mild insecticidal soap. Others, like Japanese beetles, can be pulled off by hand and then destroyed. As you will learn later in this chapter, some botanical pesticides can be harmful to fish, birds, or bees, so it is better to try a safer pest-control method first.

10. *Don't panic.* Your garden is going to be very healthy and capable of withstanding most pest attacks all by itself. Don't run for help at the sign of one or two bugs. If you see signs of pests in the garden, simply identify the problem, look in this chapter for the appropriate treatment, and carefully apply the cure. You will soon find that controlling pests in your garden is really quite simple.

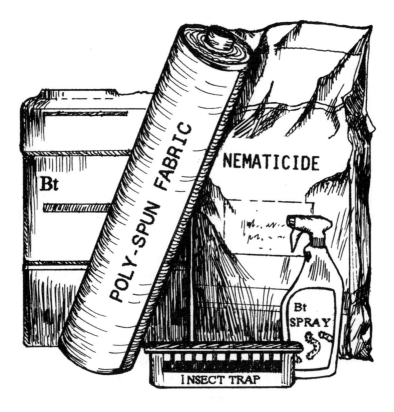

Introduction to Environmental Pest Controls

There are four main types of environmental pest control: cultural, mechanical, and biological, which are completely nontoxic, and botanical, which releases a low level of toxic material into the environment.

Cultural. Cultural pest control means creating an environment or culture in your garden that does not give pests a chance to be destructive. This incudes planting disease-resistant varieties of fruits and vegetables, keeping the garden clean and tidy, enriching the soil with natural organic fertilizer and organic matter, and adopting a proper watering program. Every gardener should do these things. A garden with an established pest-resistant culture allows plants to thrive and grow to their greatest potential, and it creates a habitat for the millions of microorganisms, worms, and beneficial insects that you want to attract.

Mechanical. Mechanical pest control means trapping the bugs and/or pulling them off your plants by hand. In the orchard chapter of this book, I suggest hanging traps in your trees to combat the flying insects that like to attack trees. Tomato hornworms, cucumber beetles, and Japanese beetles are large enough for you to pull off the plants and drop them into soapy water to kill them.

Biological. Biological pest control has to do with attracting birds, toads, ladybugs, praying mantises, and other predatory insects to come live in your garden and eat the bad, destructive bugs before they get a chance to hurt your plants.

You can now buy beneficial insects in bags from garden centers and through catalogs, and I recommend doing this. Be aware, however, that in order for the insects to stay in your garden, the garden must be in good health and have no pesticide residue. Even then, the insects can fly away and take up residence somewhere else.

Microorganisms are also used in biological pest control. *Bacillus thuringiensis,* for example, is used as an effective measure against certain pests. Commonly called *Bt,* and also known as Dipel or Thuricide, it contains bacteria that kill cabbage worms and other caterpillar pests but are nontoxic to humans.

Botanical. Botanical pest controls are mildly toxic pesticides derived from plants. Nicotine, ryania, and sabadilla are products you might hear of, but the only botanicals I recommend are rotenone and pyrethrum, which often come as a mixture in pest-control products.

Rotenone is derived from the roots of a group of tropical plants. It is effective in killing flea beetles, cucumber beetles, Colorado potato beetles, and more than fifteen other garden insects. Be aware that rotenone is toxic to fish. Some state conservation departments use rotenone to kill unwanted fish in lakes they want to restock. Please follow package instructions carefully and never use rotenone near a lake or waterway.

Pyrethrum is derived from plants in the chrysanthemum family. It is effective in controlling Japanese beetles, leafhoppers, flea beetles, and fleas.

Botanical pesticides are usually less toxic than synthetic chemical pesticides (with a few exceptions), and they are toxic for a shorter period of time. Pyrethrum and rotenone lose their toxicity within twenty-four hours of application, whereas synthetic chemical pesticides can remain toxic for days, weeks, even months. Farmers use chemicals because they kill a lot of bugs for a long time, but you can be more selective and apply your botanical pesticide only when the pests appear.

Common Pests
and Their Control

There are hundreds of bugs that can attack various kinds of garden plants. I have deliberately steered clear of recommending plants, such as potatoes, that are open invitations to bug problems.

Here is a list of insect pests, a rogues' gallery if you will, that might attack your gardens and suggestions for their control:

Aphids. Tiny, white bugs found on the leaves and stems of many plants. Spray with insecticidal soap.

Corn borers. 1-inch-long grayish-pink caterpillars. Spray or dust with rotenone or pyrethrum.

Tomato hornworm. 3- to 4-inch-long green caterpillars. Pick off or spray with Bt or pyrethrum.

Mexican bean beetles. $1/2$-inch-long bugs with yellow/brown shell with black spots usually found devouring bean plants. Spray or dust with rotenone or pyrethrum.

Japanese beetles. $1/2$-inch-long bluish-green beetle found in the northeastern, mid-Atlantic, and midwestern states. Spray or dust with rotenone or pyrethrum.

Cucumber beetles. $1/2$-inch-long greenish-yellow bugs with black heads. Spray with pyrethrum or rotenone.

Flea beetles. Tiny black insects that hop around like fleas, found perforating the leaves of eggplants and cabbages in particular. Spray or dust with rotenone or pyrethrum.

Cabbage Worms. $1^1/2$-inch-long pale green worms that arch their back as they crawl along on the leaves of cabbage plants. Spray or dust with *B. thuringiensis* var. "Berliner."

Codling moths, fruit flies, apple maggots. These are the three main insect pests that can damage the fruit if you decide to grow the Cottage Orchard in this book. These can be controlled with traps scented with pheromone lures.

Codling-moth larvae, scale insects, red bugs, and aphids. Other bugs that can damage your fruit trees. Spray your apple, plum, and cherry trees in early spring, while the trees are still dormant, with dormant oil spray, which coats the tree branches and smothers the insects.

The important thing to remember about pests is that the best cure is prevention. Keep your garden healthy, and when you do use pesticides, read the labels carefully and be cautious. A strong environmentally friendly garden will keep most bugs and diseases at bay all by itself.

PART TWO

The Garden Plans

A Cook's
Salad Garden

*O*f all the vegetables that are grown in the garden, salad vegetables are probably the most universally known and enjoyed. Even the most stubborn eater will nibble on garden-fresh tomatoes, peppers, cucumbers, and crispy lettuce drizzled with salad dressing.

Growing a salad garden is the best place to start for the beginning gardener because the chances of success are so high. All the vegetables in the salad garden are easy to grow, demand very little care, are not prone to disease or insect damage, and, face it, you already know how to make a salad.

All you need for this garden is a sunny spot about 17 feet long and 10 feet wide. You are going to grow leaf, Bibb, and romaine lettuce; spinach and arugula; tomatoes and peppers; cucumbers, onions, radishes, basil, parsley, dill, and chives.

Please read the first three chapters of this book on starting a garden, choosing tools, and controlling pests. You will then have a background of general garden knowledge and will be familiar with the terms and techniques used in this chapter.

This is a twenty-eight-week garden plan that starts in late January and keeps you involved with your garden up until the first frost in October. There will be more work to do in the busy planning months of April and May than in the slower months of July and August, but there is always a little something to do in the garden each week.

Each weekly activity list is really a "work window," meaning that you have a couple of weeks to get the chores completed. Because there are varying climates and the seasons come and go at slightly different times, each weekly work window is two to three weeks long. For instance, if you live in Springfield, Illinois, you can start your garden two to three weeks earlier than if you live in Albany, New York, but in both places the same work follows the same sequence and uses the same amount of time.

The Weekly Guide

Week One (LATE JANUARY TO FEBRUARY 1) *Order your seed catalogs.*

As soon as the Christmas and New Year's season ends, seed catalogs come pouring out of publishing houses all across the country. There are at least one hundred different seed catalogs that you can order for free or for a $1.00 to $2.00 fee. They should arrive at your house within two weeks' time, after your request.

Order two or three different catalogs so that you can have some variety in price and selection. There is a complete listing of seed catalogs in the appendix of this book, but here is a list of a few well-known catalogs:

- The Cook's Garden, Box 535, Londonderry, VT 05148
- Johnny's Selected Seeds, Foss Hill Road, Albion, ME 04901
- Nichols Garden Nursery, 1190 North Pacific Highway, Albany, OR 97321
- Park Seed Co., Cokesbury Road, Greenwood, SC 29647

Catalogs are wonderful, colorful, and a lot of fun, but you can always find a wide selection of salad garden seeds at your local lawn and garden and home center.

Week Two (EARLY FEBRUARY) *Survey friends and family.*

While you are waiting to receive your catalogs, ask your friends and family, and don't forget yourself, if they have any favorite salad greens or fixings. A lot of people have taste memories of a certain type of tomato their grandmother used to grow or a certain type of lettuce they particularly enjoy eating.

This not only gives you good ordering information, but it also gets everybody interested in the soon-to-be-planted garden. I'm going to give you my specific list of what I suggest you grow, but make a list of your own favorites and keep it ready for when the catalogs arrive.

Week Three (MID-FEBRUARY) *Choose your seeds and place your order.*

Here is a list of the types of seeds you should order to have a colorful, varied, and satisfying salad garden. You should read through your seed catalogs and pick out the seeds you like that fit into the appropriate category. For instance, you need to pick a loosehead, or leaf, lettuce. There must be twenty different types of leaf lettuce. A typical catalog offers at least four varieties. I will give you a couple of suggestions. You can follow my ideas exactly or pick something a little different.

Choose one packet each of the following varieties:

- *Leaf lettuce:* Black-Seeded Simpson, Oak Leaf, Salad Bowl,
  or Red Sails
- *Butterhead or Boston lettuce:* Nancy, Buttercrunch, Bibb, or Pirat
- *Romaine or Cos lettuce:* Valmaine, Parris Island Ços, or Rosalita
- *Spinach:* Bloomsdale Long Standing, Melody, or Tyee
- *Arugula:* Any type; also known as Rocket
- *Radish:* French breakfast, Cherry Bell, or a blend
- *Cucumber:* Marketmore, Vert de Massy, or Armenian
- *Peppers:* California Wonder, Golden Summer, or Gypsy
- *Tomatoes:* Big Boy, Celebrity, or Marmande
- *Onions:* Buy either a half pound of sets or one bunch of plants of red,
  white, or yellow
- *Basil:* Sweet Italian or Genovese
- *Dill:* Long Island or Bouquet

- *Chives and parsley:* Buy potted plants at a nursery or garden center because both chives and parsley are too difficult to grow from seed for the beginning gardener.

Be flexible when choosing your seeds. Experiment. Have fun. If you have any doubts about which seeds are best, ask the catalog representative or local garden center staff for advice. They will be happy to help you. Most seed catalogs have telephone customer service lines you can call when ordering to get the help you need.

Week Four (LATE FEBRUARY) *Choose your garden site.*

Your garden will measure 17 feet by 10 feet. Look for a site that is on level ground and gets full sunshine at least six hours every day. Be sure to avoid tall trees that will shade the area.

Your garden needs to be well drained. Look for a site that never has water puddles or standing water on it at any time of the year.

Choose a site that is fairly close to the house. You won't have so far to walk or carry items back and forth. Make sure your hose can reach the site so that you can keep the garden watered without much trouble.

Week Five (LATE FEBRUARY TO EARLY MARCH) *Choose a warm and sunny place indoors to start plants; buy seed-starting supplies.*

Next week you will start growing your tomato, pepper, cucumber, and basil plants in small containers indoors. You will need to find a place to grow them. I usually place my containers on a wide sunny windowsill or on a small card table near a sunny window.

When seeds are first planted in containers indoors, they need a warm place to germinate. Look for a place in your home that keeps a temperature of 75 to 80 degrees Fahrenheit. Kitchens tend to be warm places, or you might have a sunny bedroom that is warm.

Once the seeds have sprouted, the tiny plants need all the sunlight they can get, but they now prefer a slightly cooler temperature, about 70 degrees F.

The supplies you will need to buy include six $4^1/_2$-by-6-by-$2^1/_2$-inch plastic containers called flats, thirty-six 2-inch peat pots (peat pots are small planting pots made of dried and pressed sphagnum peat moss), one 5-pound bag of sterilized potting soil, and 3-inch marker stakes.

Week Six (EARLY TO MID-MARCH) *Start peppers and tomatoes indoors.*

You don't absolutely have to start your tomato, pepper, and basil plants indoors this week if you feel you are just too busy with other things. You can even skip this step if you want to buy tomato, pepper, and basil plants at your local garden center later in the spring. Growing them yourself is very satisfying, however, and helps bring a breath of springtime into your home. If you do want to start them, here's how.

- Gather up all your seeds and supplies. Lay down several layers of newspaper or a plastic bag to keep the table from getting messy.
- Fill the flats with potting soil and press it down with your fingers to within $1/2$ inch of the rim.
- Sprinkle about twenty seeds over the entire surface of the flat. You will end up with only six plants, but you want to plant plenty to get started.
- Cover the seeds with $1/4$ inch of additional potting soil and tamp down lightly.
- Place the flats in a pan of room-temperature water and let the flats water themselves from below. When the surface is moist, remove the flats from the water and drain.
- Write the name of the plants on the markers and stick the markers into the soil at the edge of the flat.
- Make little greenhouses by placing individual flats in separate clear plastic produce bags. This will keep the soil moist and you can watch for the seeds to sprout.
- Open the plastic-bag greenhouses every day to let in some fresh air. Lightly mist the soil if it becomes dry.
- Place the flats on cookie sheets or on cardboard to keep your table surface clean; keep the flats warm and wait.

Week Seven (MID- TO LATE MARCH) *Keep the seedlings watered and warm.*

The seedlings should begin to sprout in a week to ten days if you keep them warm enough. Cool temperatures will retard their germination, so try to protect them from cold drafts. Monitor the temperature in the room so that the room is warm enough. Make sure the soil is just moist to the touch; don't overwater. Spray the top of the soil with a little mister spray bottle of pure clean water.

Week Eight (LATE MARCH) *Thin seedlings.*

The seedlings should start to appear in about a week. As soon as they sprout, remove the plastic greenhouse. Although tiny at first, they will grow rapidly.

When the seedlings are about 1 inch tall, carefully and delicately start to thin them by pulling out sprouts so that you are left with the six largest ones spaced equally apart in the flat. The best way to do this is to pull a few, wait a few days to see which seedlings emerge as the strongest, and pull a few more of the weaker ones.

Week Nine (LATE MARCH TO EARLY APRIL) *Prepare the garden soil.*

It should be getting pretty close to springtime in your area, and the snow and winter cold should have left the soil. If you live in the South or in warmer areas of the Midwest, you may be able to start preparing your garden a little bit earlier. Clear your garden site of any rocks, leaves, branches, or other debris and begin tilling the soil.

If you feel strong and healthy, you can probably dig up the garden plot by hand. It will require quite a bit of time and back-breaking labor to get it done, though. If the labor required is too strenuous for you, I suggest you rent a rotary tiller or hire a person who digs up gardens for a living. Look in the Yellow Pages of the phone book under landscaping or look in the newspaper classified section under farm, garden, or services offered.

If your garden site is actually a lush part of your lawn, it is better if you can remove the sod before you start the garden, but that also is a lot of work. A very thorough and aggressive rotary tilling will chew up the sod very well.

Next, add four bushels of compost, humus, or composted manure to the soil along with 4 pounds of natural organic fertilizer. Till the soil one more time and rake it smooth. Now you are ready to plant.

Week Ten (LATE MARCH TO EARLY APRIL) *Begin planting lettuce, radishes, and more.*

Refer to your garden map at the beginning of this chapter and mark off eight planting rows that are 10 feet long, with 12 inches between each row. Dig the furrows, or seed trenches, $1/2$ inch deep in each row, using your finger, a stick, or the end of a long rake.

Plant the seeds only one third of a row's length: arugula in the first row, followed by radishes, leaf lettuce, Bibb lettuce, romaine lettuce, and spinach. In two weeks you will plant the next third and in another two weeks the last third.

Plant all the onion sets today, filling the whole row. One "wild card" row is left, which you can plant with whatever seeds you feel you want more of.

This method is called succession planting, which prevents the vegetables from ripening at the same time and extends your harvest over a longer period.

Sprinkle the seeds in the furrow, spacing them about $1/2$ inch apart. Cover them with $1/2$ inch of soil and tamp down. Water the area thoroughly and keep it watered until the seeds sprout.

Week Eleven (EARLY APRIL) *Keep seeds watered; transplant seedlings.*

It usually rains enough in the springtime to keep garden soil moist. But if the soil looks as if it is getting dry, set out a sprinkler and water the garden for about one-half hour at low volume.

Your tomato, pepper, and basil plants are now ready to be transplanted to peat pots. Fill the peat pots with potting soil and dig a little hole in the center with your finger. Using a spoon, carefully lift and separate the seedlings and transplant them to the new pots. Lightly press the soil around the plants and add a little more soil. Water and return to their sunny location.

Week Twelve (MID-APRIL) *Thin plants and reseed.*

The seeds you planted in the garden rows outdoors have germinated, and you can clearly see how closely they are planted. Thin them out to stand 4 inches apart by pulling out the seedlings in between. These thinnings are tiny, but they make a great addition to your salad bowl.

Now is the time to plant phase two (one-third row more) of your succession-planting scheme. Remember that each row is divided up into thirds and that you are going to seed one third of the row every two weeks to prolong the harvest season.

Smooth the row, dig a 1-inch-deep furrow, sprinkle in the seeds, cover them, press the soil down lightly, and water.

Week Thirteen (LATE APRIL TO EARLY MAY) *Begin harvesting lettuce.*

This is the moment you've been waiting for since you began your garden. You can start harvesting some of the early lettuce, spinach, and arugula. Harvest the greens that are most crowded together. Try to leave the rest of the lettuces so that they are a full 6 inches apart in the rows. While you eat the tender young plants, the rest of the lettuces can mature and grow to their full size. Remove the stems and wash and dry the lettuce. Here is a recipe.

Early Garden Green Salad

This is a salad that the French call Mesclun. It is a combination of tiny, tender salad greens tossed with a light vinaigrette dressing that allows the mild flavors of the greens to shine through.

> *4 cups salad greens, loosely packed*
>
> *2 teaspoons red or white wine vinegar (use an interesting vinegar such as tarragon white wine or raspberry red wine)*
>
> *1 teaspoon fresh lemon or lime juice*
>
> *¹/₄ teaspoon each salt and freshly ground black pepper*
>
> *1 teaspoon prepared Dijon mustard*
>
> *3 tablespoons extra-virgin olive oil*

1. Gather lettuce, arugula, and spinach leaves by thinning the rows. Remove the stems and any damaged leaves. Wash the leaves thoroughly, dry them, and keep them cool. It is important to dry the leaves or else they will stick to one another and become a clumpy mess; also, the oil won't stick to wet leaves.

2. Place the vinegar, lemon or lime juice, olive oil, mustard, salt, and pepper in the bottom of a large salad bowl. Whisk to form a creamy dressing.

3. Add the greens to the salad bowl and toss to coat evenly. Serve with crusty French bread or rolls.

Serves 4

Week Fourteen (LATE APRIL) *Continue planting; pull weeds; add mulch.*

Plant the remaining third of each row with lettuces, arugula, and spinach. Be sure to water them every other day until they germinate because there will probably be less rain falling in late April and temperatures should be warming up.

The best way to control weeds is to pull them by hand on the day after a rainfall. Be sure to get the roots as well. Pulling weeds actually helps to break up the soil in between the rows of vegetables. Cultivation of the rows by pulling weeds helps the rain penetrate the soil and aerates the soil, bringing oxygen to the microorganisms and worms, which are busy making your garden soil rich and fertile.

You don't have to pull all the weeds because you are going to put down mulch. Just pull the big ones and any that are crowding your plants in their rows.

The best way to water your garden is with a soaker hose. It is more effective and conserves water better than any other method of irrigation. Simply snake your 50-foot hose through the plants in an S pattern. A soaker hose will drench the ground 18 inches on either side of the hose, so one hose should be adequate. Leave this hose in place in the garden for the rest of the season and then attach a regular hose to it to water the garden later in the season.

Now is a good time to put a 2-inch to 4-inch layer of mulch on top of the soaker hose and between the rows. Mulch will stifle any weeds growing in your garden, conserve water, and add organic matter back to the soil. The best bet is to go to the lawn and garden center or local produce market and buy two bales of straw. Hay is all right as a substitute, but it often contains weed seeds, which will infest your garden next year.

Break off layers of straw and place it carefully between the rows and around the plants.

Week Fifteen (EARLY MAY) *Harvest radishes, arugula, and more.*

Begin harvesting radishes. Look for the largest ones or the areas that are most crowded. Pull them carefully so you don't disturb the radishes left in the row. Wash them off, remove the stems and roots, and eat them as fast as you can— they are so delicious when first pulled from the garden. Place the remainder in the refrigerator.

Harvest the arugula by pulling the entire little plant from the ground. Trim off the roots, wash the leaves and keep refrigerated. You can also snip off the arugula tops, which will be replaced by new leaves.

Harvest the leaf lettuce by pulling the whole plants, trimming the stems, washing the leaves carefully, and placing them in the refrigerator.

Arugula, Radish, and Leaf Lettuce Salad

Tangy arugula gives this fresh lettuce salad a peppery spark, and the radishes give it crunch. The sweet orange adds color and flavor.

> *1 cup arugula leaves, washed and trimmed*
>
> *3 cups leaf-lettuce leaves, washed and trimmed*
>
> *1 cup radishes, thinly sliced*
>
> *1 medium seedless orange (optional)*
>
> *1 teaspoon Dijon mustard*
>
> *1 teaspoon orange juice*
>
> *2 teaspoons lemon juice*
>
> *1 tablespoon olive oil or other salad oil*
>
> *¼ teaspoon each salt and pepper*

1. Harvest the arugula and leaf lettuce. Trim off the stems, wash, and dry. Keep cool.

2. Pull the radishes and trim off the stems and roots. Wash and slice thin.

3. Peel the orange and remove any pulp. Slice the orange across the grain into very thin slices.

4. Make the dressing by mixing the mustard, orange and lemon juices, olive oil, and salt and pepper in a salad bowl. Whisk to form a creamy mixture.

5. Add the orange slices, toss them in the dressing, and then remove them.

6. Add the radishes, arugula, and lettuce. Toss to coat well. Arrange the orange slices around the salad and serve.

Serve 4

Week Sixteen (MID- TO LATE MAY) *Plant tomatoes, peppers, basil, herbs, and cucumbers.*

Except in the coldest northern regions, you should no longer be worried about getting nighttime frosts that might kill your young tomato, pepper, or basil plants. It is best to transplant on a cloudy, windless day if you can wait for one; if not, wait until late afternoon so that the transplants don't suffer in the hot sun all day.

Plant the tomatoes in a grid pattern. You have room in the garden for only six plants, so pick out the healthiest ones. Plant them in two rows of three, $2^1/_2$ feet apart in each direction.

Dig a hole for the plants and loosen the soil. Place the plant into the soil at a depth slightly below its level in the pot. Mound soil up $^1/_2$ to 1 inch around the stem and press down firmly with your hands. Water thoroughly.

Plant the peppers in a row running parallel to the tomatoes. Space them 2 feet apart in every direction.

Plant the cucumbers in two circles about 3 feet across. Rake smooth two large circles about 3 feet in diameter. Plant individual cucumber seeds in a pentagonal or hexagonal formation across the circles. Place one or two in the center also. Cover with $^1/_2$ inch of soil and firm it with the palms of your hands.

Plant the basil plants, and any flats of chives and parsley that you may have bought at the local nursery or garden center, by interspersing them around the perimeter of the tomato and pepper plants along the edge of the garden.

Plant the dill seeds by digging a 2-foot-long furrow along the edge of the garden near the cucumbers and then sprinkling in a few seeds spaced $^1/_2$ inch apart. Cover the seeds with $^1/_2$ inch of soil, firm down, and water.

Water the entire planting area thoroughly and take a rest.

Week Seventeen (LATE MAY) *Harvest spinach.*

Now is the time to harvest the first planting of spinach you made a few weeks ago. Pull the plants up by the roots, remove the roots and stems, and wash the leaves thoroughly, as dirt and sand can easily get embedded in the crinkly leaves. Dry and place in a bag in the refrigerator until you are ready to make your spinach salad.

Spinach Salad
with Creamy Dressing

4 to 6 cups spinach leaves
1 cup fresh mushrooms, thinly sliced
1 cup unflavored croutons
¼ cup light or regular mayonnaise
¼ cup yogurt or sour cream
2 tablespoons wine vinegar or lemon juice
salt and pepper to taste

1. Save three large spinach leaves for the dressing and place the rest in a large salad bowl.

2. Add the sliced mushrooms and croutons to the spinach.

3. Make the dressing by placing the three reserved spinach leaves, the mayonnaise, sour cream, vinegar, salt, and pepper in a food processor or blender. Whir to form a creamy dressing.

4. Pour the dressing over the spinach salad and toss to coat well.

5. Feel free to add radishes to this salad if you like.

Serves 4

Week Eighteen (EARLY JUNE) *Mulch the garden.*

It is important to let the soil in your garden become thoroughly warm before you mulch around tomatoes and peppers. If the ground is still too cool, spreading mulch on top may stunt the growth of the plants and lead to disease. Unless you are experiencing an excessively cold, wet spring, the ground is usually warm and dry enough to mulch two weeks after you transplant the tomatoes and peppers out to the open garden.

Spread a 4-inch layer of straw or other favorite mulch around and between the tomato, pepper, and basil plants. Be sure to mulch around the other herb plants and the cucumbers if they are up and growing. Put mulch between the plants and the rows between the plants. Look over at the other rows of the garden and apply additional mulch on them or any other bare spot where the soil is peeking through.

Mulch helps to keep weeds out of the garden, acts to trap moisture in the soil, and as it decays, adds valuable organic matter to the soil.

Week Nineteen (EARLY JUNE) *Support tomatoes.*

Not all gardeners prefer to support their tomato plants off the ground with stakes or cages. Many like to let their tomato plants grow naturally in a very bushy form with the vines trailing across the ground. This method will produce a great crop, but it is unsightly and can lead to the spread of disease. I have always used stakes and cages to hold up my tomatoes, and I suggest you do the same, especially in this tidy little salad garden of limited space. Here's how.

Buy premade tomato cages at the lawn and garden center. You should have no problem buying them in early June, but it might be a good idea to buy them earlier in the season to be sure they are in stock. As a subway conductor used to announce at every stop during the holiday season, "Do your shopping early so you get what you want to buy." Get the heavy-gauge ones, which can cost up to $2.00 or $3.00 apiece. They should stand about 4 feet high.

Arrange the cages over the tomato plants, poking the stakes into the ground around the tomato plant stem but keeping them 3 to 4 inches away from the stem in each direction.

Week Twenty (MID-JUNE) *Control pests; harvest romaine.*

Now is the time when tomato plants and sometimes pepper plants start getting attacked by the tomato hornworm. Check your tomato and pepper plants for green caterpillars about 2 to 4 inches long. Pick them off by hand and squash them or spray the plants with *Bt* or rotenone. Always follow package instructions when handling pesticides and be sure to read the chapter in this book on pesticide use.

Pick a couple heads of romaine lettuce, trim off the stalks and roots, and wash carefully. Place in a plastic bag and keep cool in the refrigerator.

Romaine Caesar Salad

Caesar salad is named after a restaurateur from Tijuana, Mexico. The key ingredient is fresh, crispy romaine lettuce. This Caesar salad does not contain the traditional raw egg because of health concerns over the safety of eating uncooked eggs.

> *4 to 6 cups romaine lettuce, coarsely chopped*
>
> *2 cups large unflavored croutons or chunks of crusty French bread, lightly toasted*
>
> *2 anchovy filets*
>
> *1 clove garlic*
>
> *2 tablespoons lemon juice*
>
> *5 tablespoons olive oil*
>
> *¼ cup grated Parmesan cheese*
>
> *freshly ground black pepper to taste but no salt*

1. Harvest the romaine lettuce, trim off the stalks, and separate the leaves. Wash and dry the leaves carefully and chop them into bite-sized pieces.

2. Place the anchovy filets in the bottom of a large salad bowl. Peel and mash the garlic clove and add it to the bowl. Mash the anchovy and the garlic to form a coarse paste.

3. Add the lemon juice and olive oil to the anchovy-garlic paste and whisk to form a creamy dressing.

4. Add the romaine to the dressing and toss to coat well. Add the cheese and toss again. Add the croutons and toss again but only at the last minute because you want the croutons to be coated, not soggy.

5. Add the black pepper and serve.

Serves 4

Week Twenty-one (LATE JUNE) *Harvest Bibb lettuce, early onions, and herbs.*

Bibb lettuce takes the longest to mature of all the lettuces. If you have kept the plants watered and have given them enough room to grow, you should have perfect heads of lettuce that look as good or better than lettuces you find at fancy gourmet stores.

Pull the Bibb lettuce from the ground. Trim off the root and stems and peel away any lower leaves that look damaged. Wash the heads carefully, place them in a plastic bag, and keep them refrigerated.

Your onions are ready to eat now, too. Pull only the onions that you are going to eat immediately. Trim off the stalks and stems and wash off the dirt.

Use scissors or a sharp knife to trim off the chives, parsley, and dill that you want to use. All of these will keep for a week in the refrigerator if they are washed and placed in a plastic bag.

Spring Green Salad with Herbs and Onions

> *2 heads Bibb lettuce*
> *2 cups assorted garden greens such as arugula or spinach*
> *2 medium onions*
> *¼ cup chopped fresh herbs: basil, dill, chives, and parsley*
> *1 teaspoon Dijon mustard*
> *1 tablespoon white wine vinegar*
> *3 tablespoons olive oil or other salad oil*
> *salt and pepper to taste*

1. Harvest the heads of Bibb lettuce, trim the stems, break the leaves apart, and wash well. Dry and keep cool.

2. Harvest the arugula and spinach; trim, wash, and dry.

3. Harvest the onions; trim off the stalks and the roots. Peel the outer skins and wash. Slice the onions very thin and reserve.

4. Pick a few sprigs of each of the four herbs you planted earlier in the spring. Trim off any flowers or flower buds and discard. Wash, chop, and reserve.

5. Make the dressing in a large salad bowl. Place the mustard, vinegar, salt, and pepper in the bottom of the bowl and stir. Add the oil and whisk to form a creamy dressing.

6. Break the lettuce, arugula, and spinach into bite-sized chunks and add to the salad bowl. Sprinkle with the herbs and toss to coat well.

Serves 4

Week Twenty-two (MID-JULY) *Harvest cucumbers; add a little fertilizer; keep the garden watered.*

Don't wait for your cucumbers to get too large before you pick them. Larger cucumbers can be full of seeds, and they can be bitter. Choose smaller ones and simply slip them off the vines. Wash them a little and keep them in the refrigerator.

If you have had a bumper crop of cucumbers and you really want to make pickles, go ahead. Any type of cucumber can be pickled.

Mid-July is a time of the year when rain is scarce, so it is important for you to keep your garden watered. The best way to water is with a soaker or drip-irrigation hose. Buy a 50-foot soaker hose and snake it through the garden up and down the rows and through the plants in a large S curve. Bury the hose under the mulch and leave it there for the entire summer.

Attach a regular extension hose to the soaker and run that hose back to the spigot. Turn on the water and let it run for two to four hours, which gives the garden a slow, deep watering that is much better than a short, fast watering.

Water the garden no more than once a week at this time of year. You can remove the soaker hose each time you use it, or just leave it in place. They are not unattractive.

Cucumbers with Sour Cream and Dill

It is hard to get a meal in a Scandinavian country in the summer that doesn't include this dish. If you prefer, use chives or parsley instead of dill for a cooling summer salad.

> *2 medium-sized cucumbers*
> *1 cup sour cream*
> *1 tablespoon lemon juice*
> *1/4 cup fresh dill, minced, plus several dill sprigs for garnish*
> *salt and pepper to taste*

1. Wash and peel the cucumbers. Slice them lengthwise into quarters. Scoop out any seeds and discard. Slice the cucumbers thinly or dice them.

2. In a medium salad bowl, mix the sour cream with the lemon juice, minced dill, salt, and pepper. Add the cucumbers and stir to blend well.

3. Let the cucumber salad rest for at least thirty minutes for the flavors to mingle. Garnish with the dill sprigs and serve.

Serves 4 to 6

Week Twenty-three (MID- TO LATE JULY) *Harvest tomatoes and peppers.*

Red, ripe, juicy tomatoes and crisp, green bell peppers are what most people dream about when they think about a garden. Tomatoes are America's favorite vegetable (even though they're technically a fruit), and none taste better than those you grow yourself.

Don't wait for your tomatoes to get so ripe that they fall off the vine before you pick them. I like to pick mine a couple of days early and let them ripen up in my kitchen. Ripe tomatoes will be red and will come right off the vine with a slight tug.

Harvest green peppers as soon as you feel they are large enough to eat. They usually need just a slight twist to remove them from the plant. Red peppers are green peppers that are left on the plant. Also, once green peppers are picked, they will begin to turn red.

Mediterranean Salad

Since the Spanish brought tomatoes and peppers back from the New World, this salad and all its variations have been served throughout the Mediterranean countries of Spain, France, Italy, Greece, the Levant, and North Africa.

> *3 medium-sized ripe tomatoes*
> *2 medium-sized ripe green or red bell peppers*
> *1 medium cucumber*
> *1 medium onion*
> *1 head romaine lettuce*
> *extra-virgin olive oil and red wine vinegar*
> *salt and pepper to taste*

1. Slice the tomatoes, peppers, cucumbers, and onion into thin slices.

2. Separate the leaves of a head of romaine lettuce. Wash and dry the leaves carefully. Lay them flat on a large serving plate to make a bed for the rest of the vegetables.

3. Arrange the vegetable slices in clusters or alternate them to form an attractive display.

4. Drizzle olive oil and red wine vinegar over the vegetables; sprinkle with salt and pepper and serve.

Variations: Add a can of solid white tuna in water or oil, black olives, capers, feta cheese, or other of your favorites to give the salad your own special appeal.

Serves 4

Week Twenty-four (EARLY AUGUST) *Pinch basil blossoms; harvest basil.*

What you want from your basil plants are the bright-green fleshy leaves. When the plants begin to flower, the leaves stop growing, and the plants start to die. Continue to keep the blossoms pinched off during the summer until you are ready to harvest the basil.

To harvest basil, cut the top stems off, leaving a strong central stalk and several side shoots. The remaining plant will regenerate more leaves and shoots. Pull the leaves off the stems, wash them, place them in a plastic bag, and keep refrigerated until ready to use.

Linguine with Fresh Basil Pesto Sauce

1 pound linguine
2 cups packed fresh basil leaves, chopped
$^1/_3$ cup unsalted walnuts, sunflower seeds, or pine nuts
1 large clove garlic, peeled and chopped
$^1/_3$ cup grated Parmesan cheese
$^1/_2$ cup pure or light olive oil

1. Cook the pasta in a large pot of boiling water, following package instructions, usually about eight to ten minutes. (Reserve $^1/_2$ cup of the cooking water; then drain the pasta.)

2. While the pasta is cooking, make the pesto. Place the basil leaves, nuts, and garlic in a food processor. Pulse to mince fine. Add the cheese and pulse to blend well. Slowly add the olive oil to form a creamy paste.

3. Toss the pasta with the $^1/_2$ cup reserved cooking water and the pesto. Serve immediately.

Serves 4

Week Twenty-five (LATE AUGUST) *Replant lettuce, arugula, and spinach.*

Lettuce, arugula, and spinach prefer growing in the cool of spring, but if you plant some now and keep them watered until they germinate, you can have a lovely salad crop on into the cool days in fall.

Clear the garden rows of any debris. Remove the mulch and keep it nearby to return to the rows later. Dig a bushel of compost into the rows you want to replant and turn the soil over very well.

Dig planting furrows $^1/_2$ inch deep and 10 feet long. Sprinkle the rows with the seeds you want to replant, cover with soil, and firm down. Keep the seeds watered until they germinate; then weed, cultivate, and thin the plantings and return the mulch, just as you did in the spring.

Week Twenty-six (EARLY SEPTEMBER) *Continue harvesting tomatoes, peppers, and onions.*

Your garden will be moving full steam ahead ripening tomatoes, peppers, and other vegetables. Be sure to keep picking even if you can't eat it all. Your plants will produce better and be healthier if you keep them picked. Remove and discard any tomatoes that fall from the plants and begin to rot.

If you have more produce than you can eat, set up a produce stand for your kids and sell some to passersby, or give the produce away to friends, neighbors, or a community food bank.

If you are really ambitious, you might want to can tomatoes or make tomato soup or salsa or even ketchup. Check your local library or cooperative extension agency for recipes and instructions.

Pasta Primavera

This recipe is for the original healthful pasta primavera made without heavy cream. If you want to add cream, by all means do so, but these fresh garden vegetables are so delicious you might not want to.

> *1 pound pasta such as fusilli, bow ties, or ziti*
> *3 tablespoons olive oil*
> *1 medium onion, peeled and chopped*
> *1 medium red or green bell pepper, seeds removed and chopped*
> *3 large ripe tomatoes, cored and chopped*
> *1 clove garlic, peeled and minced*
> *2 tablespoons each minced basil and parsley*
> *salt and pepper to taste*
> *grated Parmesan or Romano cheese to taste*

1. Cook the pasta in a large pot of boiling water for eight to ten minutes. Drain and keep warm.

2. While the pasta is cooking, you have time to make the sauce. Heat the olive oil in a heavy pot and add the onions and peppers. Saute for three minutes, stirring often.

3. Add the tomatoes, garlic, salt, and pepper. Cook over medium heat for five minutes.

4. Add the basil and parsley, stir, and serve over the hot pasta. Sprinkle with grated cheese.

Serves 4

Week Twenty-seven (MID-SEPTEMBER) *Savoring this year; planning for next.*

Now that the gardening season is just about over, it is a good time to jot down some of the successes and some of the failures you have had. Here are some questions you might ask yourself to help make your gardening a better experience next time around:

- Which plants grew the best? the worst?
- Did you grow enough to eat as much as you wanted? Did you grow too much? What did you do with the excess?
- Did you have any unusual problems with diseases, drought, or pest attacks?
- How would you improve the garden next year?

Late Summer Salad

This is a good old-fashioned mixed salad made with whatever looks fresh and tasty in the garden.

> *1 to 2 heads lettuce*
> *1 bunch each arugula and spinach*
> *2 tomatoes*
> *1 green bell pepper*
> *1 onion*
> *$^1/_4$ cup minced herbs*
> *$^1/_2$ cup vinegar and oil dressing*

1. Wash the lettuce leaves, arugula, and spinach. Dry and keep cool.
2. Chop the tomatoes, pepper, and onion.
3. Add all the ingredients to a large salad bowl. Toss and serve.

Serves 4

Week Twenty-eight (LATE SEPTEMBER TO FIRST FROST) *Start getting ready for the season's end.*

Sometime after Labor Day the nights begin to cool, the days shorten, and the garden begins to slow down production. You will still have some tomatoes and peppers, herbs, and perhaps salad greens if you replanted, but your cucumbers should be long gone.

A heavy frost will kill your tomato, pepper, and basil plants. You can protect them by laying a light blanket or cloth over the plants at night when the weatherman predicts a frost. Just remove the blanket during the day and return it to the plants on frosty nights.

Once the weather turns cold, however, your plants will die. Remove all dead plants from the garden and throw them on your compost pile. Spread a layer of any compost you have on hand, as well as any straw you have left, over the garden. Rake a layer of leaves over your garden to protect it during the winter. All of this organic matter will begin to decay and return to the soil over the winter. In spring you can till up your garden and incorporate all of this valuable organic matter into the soil.

A Kitchen Herb Garden

A Kitchen Herb Garden is the easiest garden described in this book for you to grow. Measuring only 6 feet wide by 10 feet long, it is also the smallest garden and is very flexible. If your garden space is narrower and longer than the space I recommend, you can easily reconfigure the garden's shape.

Growing an herb garden is easy because the proliferation of herb bedding plants at lawn and garden centers gives you the option of simply buying the herb plants you need rather than planting everything from seed.

From a horticultural point of view, an herb garden is also easy because it is virtually pest-free; in fact, many people swear that herbs can actually deter insect pests from the garden. An herb garden requires very little in the way of fertilizer and not much watering. Once you get it established, it seems to take care of itself quite nicely.

The Kitchen Herb Garden is also one of the most satisfying gardens to grow. The flavors of fresh herbs are so much more wonderful than dried ones, although the herbs you dry yourself are a cook's bonus that you will get to enjoy during the dead of winter. The blooms of herbs can be just as beautiful as flowers; in fact, herbs in flower make a lovely bouquet.

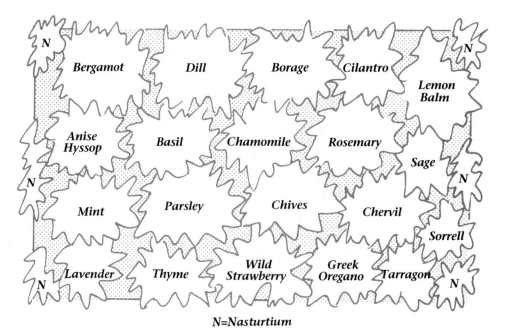

N=Nasturtium

My recommendations for a Kitchen Herb Garden include both annual and perennial herbs to use fresh or dried in cooking, to infuse into your own herb teas, and to make fragrant potpourri. You will find complete instructions for planting and harvesting the herbs, seven recipes for cooking with fresh herbs, directions for drying herbs, a recipe for herb tea, and pointers on how to make potpourri.

If you want to grow herbs only for cooking, simply don't plant the herbs recommended for tea and potpourri—you might want to try them next year. Here's what you will be growing:

- Culinary herbs: basil, chervil, cilantro, chives, dill, Greek oregano, nasturtium, parsley, rosemary, sage, tarragon, savory, and thyme
- Tea herbs: anise hyssop, borage, chamomile, lemon balm, mint, and wild strawberry
- Potpourri herbs: bergamot and lavender (rosemary, mint, anise hyssop, and chamomile are also potpourri herbs)

The Weekly Guide

Week One (EARLY TO MID-FEBRUARY) *Order seed catalogs.*

Any seed catalog will offer an adequate selection of herb seeds and some herb plants to order by mail, but not every catalog will offer every herb you might want to buy. Here are a few catalogs that have developed a reputation for an extensive herb selection:

- Fox Hill Farm, 444 West Michigan Avenue, Parma, MI 49269
- Herb Gathering, Inc., 5742 Kenwood, Kansas City, MO 64110
- Meadowsweet Herb Farm, 729 Mt. Holly Road, North Shrewsbury, VT 05738
- Nichols Garden Nursery, 1190 North Pacific Highway, Albany, OR 97321
- Shepherd's Garden Seeds, 30 Irene Street, Torrington, CT 06790
- Taylor Herb Gardens, Inc., 1535 Lone Oak Road, Vista, CA 92084

Week Two (MID-FEBRUARY) *Visit your local garden center.*

While you are waiting for your catalogs to arrive, it's a good idea to stop by one or two of your local garden centers. Browse through their selection of herb seeds on display and check to see if they have small boxes of fertilizer and seed-starting supplies such as peat pots and potting soil. Ask the salesperson how many of the herbs listed above they will stock as bedding plants.

Week Three (LATE FEBRUARY) *Place your order.*

Now is the time to place your catalog order or go ahead and buy the seed packets you want from the lawn and garden center. It is not unusual for companies to be out of stock on herbs if you wait too long.

Because herbs have so many common names, I have added the scientific name to better identify them. Choose one packet each of the following varieties:

- Anise hyssop (*Agastache foeniculum*): Perennial, 2 feet. Also known as licorice mint. Delicate anise-flavored leaves are good for tea. Hard to find as bedding plant. Start indoors.

- Bergamot (*Monarda didyma*): Perennial, 2 feet. Also known as bee balm and Oswego tea. Delicate orange-flavored leaves good for tea. Flowers attract bees and hummingbirds. Start indoors.

- Lemon balm (*Melissa officinalis*): Perennial, 2 feet. Lemony leaves are good for tea. You might find lemon balm as a bedding plant, but be prepared to start indoors.

- Greek oregano (*Origanum heracleoticum*): Perennial, 6 inches. Most of the so-called oregano plants you buy at garden centers are really pot marjoram, which does not have the distinctive flavor of Greek oregano. Shepherd's and Meadowsweet Herb Farm are good sources.

Start the following outdoors:

- Borage (*Borago officinalis*): Annual, 2 feet. Leaves taste of cucumber. Good for teas and for salad. Plant seeds in the garden.

- Chamomile (*Matricaria chamomilla* or *M. rectita*): Annual, 12 to 18 inches. Small, daisylike flowers make a soothing apple-flavored tea. Plant seeds in the garden.

- Chervil (*Anthriscus cerefolium*): Annual, 10 inches. Feathery, lacy leaves give anise/parsley flavor to potato and other salads. Very popular in France. Sow seeds in the garden.

- Cilantro (*Coriandrum sativum*): Annual, 12 to 18 inches. Also called fresh coriander and Chinese parsley. Adds tang to salsa, stir-fries, and Indian foods. Doesn't dry well. Plant in garden soil.
- Dill (*Anethum graveolens*): Annual, 18 to 24 inches. Minced dill leaves give flavor to steamed carrots, gravlax, and cucumber salad. Look for the new Fernleaf dill. Plant seeds in the garden.
- Nasturtium (*Tropaeolum majus*): Annual, 6 to 12 inches. Nasturtium is really a colorful flower, but its leaves taste like watercress. I always ring my herb garden with nasturtiums, and I think you should, too. Plant seeds in the garden.

The remaining herbs for this garden—basil, chives, parsley, rosemary, sage, tarragon, sorrel, thyme, and wild strawberry—are all easily bought as bedding plants at your local garden center. Of course, if you feel ambitious, all these herbs can be started from seed indoors, and seed packets are readily available through catalogs or at garden centers.

Week Four (LATE FEBRUARY TO EARLY MARCH) *Choose your garden site.*

An herb garden needs at least six to eight hours of full sun each day, and more is better. An herb garden can tolerate some partial shade, but not much. The more shade it gets, the less profusion of leaf and bloom you will get. Now is a good time to remove interfering tree limbs or shrubbery to give your herb garden the room and sun it needs.

Look for a sunny spot along a fence or up against the house to give the garden an attractive and protective back wall. Just outside the kitchen door is ideal, as long as it gets plenty of sun. Of course, you can redesign this garden any way you want. Circular or sundial patterns are very popular, as are four-square grid patterns.

Week Five (EARLY MARCH) *Start seeds indoors.*

It is usually difficult to find anise hyssop, bergamot, and Greek oregano already started as transplants at garden centers. These are really wonderful herbs for your garden, so you need to start them indoors, which is easy. The only space needed is a sunny windowsill large enough to hold a few small flowerpots.

First, buy or borrow three 4-inch flowerpots, either plastic or ceramic, and a small bag of sterilized potting soil. You will also need a spray-mist watering bottle.

Next, fill the pots with soil four-fifths full. Sprinkle four or five seeds of one variety in one pot and repeat with the other two pots. A packet of seed contains enough seeds to plant and grow fifty or sixty of each variety, but what are you going to do with that many? If you want to plant more pots of each variety, go ahead; you can always share your seedlings with friends or swap them with other gardeners. Sprinkle a light layer of soil over the seeds, no more than $^1/_{32}$ or at most $^1/_{16}$ inch of soil. Press down lightly and spray lightly with water.

Make three mini-greenhouses out of three plastic supermarket produce bags. Place a pot in a plastic bag, gather the bag opening, and secure it with a twist tie. These faux greenhouses help retain moisture and warmth, the two critical elements of successful seed starting. Place the pots on a sunny windowsill.

Week Six (EARLY TO MID-MARCH) *Keep pots warm and watered.*

Every two or three days, check your pots and give them a light misting of water. Feel the pots and be sure that they are warm, not cool, to the touch. It usually takes from a week to ten days for seeds to germinate and sprout. Once they do, remove the plastic bags and keep the seedlings lightly watered.

Week Seven (MID- TO LATE MARCH) *Prepare the garden.*

As I mentioned earlier in this chapter, this garden is only 6 feet deep and 10 feet long, which is plenty of room for a delightful herb garden.

Remove any sticks, sod, rocks, or debris from the garden site.

Dig up the area by hand with a forked spade or till it with a rotary tiller. Add a 4- to 6-inch layer of organic matter such as compost, shredded leaves, or composted manure, and 1 pound of natural organic fertilizer and dig all of that into the soil. Rake the soil smooth and you are ready to plant.

Week Eight (LATE MARCH) *Plant cool-weather herbs in the garden.*

Depending on the kind of weather you've been having in your part of the country, you should be ready to plant borage, chamomile, chervil, cilantro, and dill directly in the garden this week. Please refer to the garden design described at the beginning of this chapter to know where you should plant what. Dill, borage, and cilantro can grow 2 feet high, so you want to place them in the back. Chamomile grows 12 inches high, so you want to put that in the middle row, whereas lower-growing chervil (about 10 inches) should be in the front row.

Instead of planting straight, narrow rows, plant small areas of these herbs. Smooth out and mark three herb areas, approximately 2 feet by 2 feet each, in the center and on either side of the back row of your herb garden. Form your hands into claws and poke shallow holes into each herb area no more than $1/4$ to $1/2$ inch deep. Scatter the dill seeds over one area, the borage seeds over another, and the cilantro seeds over the third. Using the palm of your hand, smooth out the holes you made and pat the soil down over the areas you just planted. Repeat this process with the chamomile in the middle row and the chervil in the front row.

After all the seeds are planted, water the areas with a watering can. Keep the soil moist until the seeds germinate in a week to ten days.

Week Nine (EARLY APRIL) *Buy bedding herbs from a garden center.*

Although it is not time to plant these seedlings outside in the garden yet, it is a good time to buy them now for two reasons: to be sure you get the best selection of what you want and to get them acclimated to the conditions in your yard. The plants you buy have been grown in a greenhouse and then shipped to a garden center, so they need a chance to get adjusted to their new surroundings before being planted outdoors. Place them in a partially shaded and protected spot outdoors and keep them watered. Most garden centers sell herbs in packs of four or six, but a number of centers sell individual plants. Ask if you can mix and match your herb selections.

Here is a list of bedding herbs:

- Basil (*Ocimum basilicum*): Annual, 12 to 24 inches. You can often buy basil scented with cinnamon, lemon, or anise, and some with large and some with tiny leaves. Grow whichever kind you like, but I suggest buying two large-leafed green basil plants for making pesto and for drying and two to three tiny "piccolo" or mini-basil, which are great for pizza, pasta, and tomato dishes.

- Chives (*Allium schoenoprasum*): Perennial, 12 inches. Chives are the delicately flavored member of the onion family. A classic on baked potato and in omelets, chives also have beautiful purple flowers.

- Lavender (*Lavandula angustifolia*): Perennial, 18 to 36 inches. Look for the compact 'Munstead' variety or the L. latifolia strain if you can find it. English or French lavender can grow as high as 3 feet and can get out of hand. Both varieties send out lovely flowers that make great potpourri.

- Mint (*Mentha spicata*): Perennial, 2 feet. In the nineteenth century no Southern home would be complete without a spearmint bed for flavoring bourbon drinks like mint julep. If you prefer more spice, you could grow peppermint, M. piperita. Both types are good for fresh mint tea, the beverage of choice in many Arab countries, and potpourri. Buy one plant.

- Parsley (*Petroselinum crispum*): Biennial, 12 inches. Parsley grows for two years and then dies, although it often reseeds itself. Choose two to three plants of either curled or flat-leaf Italian parsley or both.

- Rosemary (*Rosemarinus officinalis*): 12 to 18 inches. When I lived in Spain, our driveway was lined by a 30-foot-long hedge of rosemary. We would hack off branches and toss it on the coals of the barbacoa to flavor chicken and fish. In California and other warm climates, rosemary is grown as a perennial that can grow over 2 feet tall, but in cooler climates it is treated as an annual. One plant will be enough.

- Sage (*Salvia officinalis*): Perennial, 2 feet. Dusty gray-green sage leaves are a classic complement to turkey and poultry dishes. Sage is also common in Italian cream sauces, especially with ravioli. Buy one plant.

- Sorrel (*Rumex acetosa*): Perennial, 12 to 16 inches. Also called French sorrel, sorrel is a low-growing plant with broad green leaves that taste of tangy lemon. Sorrel leaves are a wonderful addition to salads and sauces, but they do not dry well. Buy one or two plants.

- French tarragon (*Artemisia dracunculus var. 'Sativa'*): Perennial, 2 feet. Be sure to look for graceful true French tarragon with its peppery/anise flavor as opposed to the rank, tasteless Russian tarragon carried in some garden centers. Wonderful for flavoring wine vinegar and vinaigrette, sauces, and roasted, fried, or grilled chicken. Buy one plant.

- Thyme (*Thymus vulgaris*): Perennial, 12 inches. Also known as English thyme, thyme is a hardy little plant that spreads well, is easy to use fresh or dry, and gives a wonderful flavor to grilled meats and marinades. Buy one plant.

- Wild Strawberry (*Fragaria rosacea*): Perennial, 10 inches. Also called Alpine strawberry. Wild strawberry leaves are good in teas and potpourri, and the tiny berries are delicious to eat. A lovely little plant that is also a good ground cover.

Week Ten (MID-APRIL) *Thin indoor seedlings.*

Your bergamot, anise hyssop, and Greek oregano seeds have sprouted by now, and you probably have a few seedlings growing in each pot. Carefully remove all but one or two of the strongest seedlings in each pot. Water and keep warm.

Week Eleven (LATE APRIL) *Weed; prepare garden for transplants.*

A few weeds are probably popping up in your garden already, and they may be crowding or smothering the dill, cilantro, chervil, borage and chamomile you planted there. Pull them out and keep your seedlings watered. Remove any leaves, weeds, or other debris that may have accumulated in the rest of the herb bed.

Week Twelve (EARLY MAY) *Harvest early herbs.*

If the weather has cooperated and you have kept your seedlings watered, you now have some first-of-spring dill, chervil, and cilantro herbs to harvest and use in cooking. You won't have a lot of any one herb, so the best thing to do is make an omelet *aux fines herbes*.

Omelet aux Fines Herbes

This recipe makes enough for one omelet. If you plan to make more, simply multiply the ingredients and be sure to have plenty of fresh herbs already minced to add to the eggs. With a salad and a loaf of French bread, this makes a delightful luncheon or light supper.

2 large eggs
2 tablespoons water
$1/2$ teaspoon prepared Dijon mustard
a pinch each salt and pepper to taste
1 tablespoon minced fresh chervil and dill
1 teaspoon unsalted butter or margarine

1. Trim off a few sprigs each of dill and chervil. Rinse them lightly and dry them with a paper towel. Mince them finely with a knife and reserve.

2. Whisk the eggs, water, mustard, salt, pepper, and herbs together in a medium bowl.

3. Place an omelet pan over medium heat for one minute. Add the butter or margarine and swirl to coat the bottom of the pan.

4. Add the egg mixture and let rest for ten seconds. Use a spatula to dig little trenches in the eggs from the outside of the pan toward the center. Tilt the pan to allow the uncooked egg to flow into the little trenches.

5. When the omelet has begun to set, fold it over itself and transfer it to a warmed plate.

Serves 1

Week Thirteen (MID-MAY) *Set out transplants.*

Please refer to the garden plan described at the beginning of this chapter to spot where each of your herb transplants is supposed to go. Naturally you can change the plan if you wish, but, once again, remember that taller plants should be in the back row and shorter plants in the front.

Walk around the garden and place the potted herbs on their respective planting sites. Using a small hand trowel, dig a hole slightly larger than the root ball of the transplant. Remove any rocks or twigs and break up any clumps of soil. Holding the plant carefully, turn the pot upside down and gently squeeze the pot. This should loosen the root ball, and the plant should slip out of the pot. Place the plant into the hole even with or slightly below the soil surface. Gather the soil around and tamp it down firmly with your hand. Repeat with all the other plants and give each a good watering.

Week Fourteen (LATE MAY) *Plant nasturtiums.*

Nasturtiums are low-growing, carefree plants with lovely flowers and foliage. Their seeds are as large as corn kernels. Place as many as four to six seeds around the outside of the garden, one at each corner and maybe a couple more here and there. Simply poke the seeds down into the ground about an inch deep. Cover the hole and tamp down. Nasturtium leaves and blossoms are edible and are commonly used in salads in California-style restaurants.

Week Fifteen (LATE MAY TO EARLY JUNE) *Mulch the herb garden.*

Mulch is a very effective way to control weeds, conserve water, and add organic matter to your garden. I suggest using a mixture of compost and peat moss or finely shredded tree bark and peat moss as your mulch. This is a pretty little garden, and you wouldn't want to spoil its good looks by mulching with something as coarse as hay, straw, or shredded leaves. You will need one 4-cubic-foot bag of sphagnum peat moss and one comparably sized bag of compost or shredded bark.

Simply spread the mulch 2 to 4 inches thick over the entire soil surface of the garden and around each area of herb plants. Pull out any weeds that may have sprouted up till now and add a little more mulch later in the summer if weeds begin to pop through.

Week Sixteen (EARLY JUNE) *Harvest herbs.*

June is a wonderful time for a fresh garden salad. There are plenty of interesting lettuces available, and your herbs are ready for a little pruning. Harvest your salad herbs by pinching off the topmost leaves of sage and basil and the outer leaves of sorrel. It doesn't matter where you harvest the chives from. Harvesting helps the herbs get bushy and more productive.

Mesclun Salad with Fresh Herbs

Mesclun is the French name for an early summer salad of mixed greens and herbs. Shop your farmer's market or grocery for a colorful selection of salad greens such as arugula, red and green leaf lettuce, mache, or whatever looks good to you. Your fresh herbs will make this salad as good as any served in the south of France.

> *4 to 5 cups fresh salad greens*
> *6 to 8 leaves each sorrel, basil, and sage*
> *12 to 15 long, slender chive sprigs*
> *2 tablespoons lemon juice, or balsamic or red wine vinegar*
> *¼ cup extra-virgin or virgin olive oil*
> *salt and pepper to taste*

1. Wash and dry the fresh salad greens and reserve.

2. Wash and dry the herbs and reserve.

3. Pour the lemon juice or vinegar, olive oil, salt, and pepper into a large salad bowl and whisk together to form a creamy dressing. Add the salad greens and toss to coat well.

4. Pile the greens onto individual salad plates and tuck the sorrel, basil, and sage leaves into each pile. Crisscross the chive sprigs on top and serve.

Serves 4

Week Seventeen (MID-JUNE) *Harvest herbs for tea.*

Harvesting herbs for making herb tea is one of the easiest things you can do to enjoy the fruits of your herb garden. Just snip off a few of the top buds, leaves, or flowers, all of which make good tea.

Fresh Herb Tea

The herbs you have planted for tea include anise hyssop, borage, chamomile, lemon balm, mint, and wild strawberry. Simply place fresh herbs in a teapot, fill the pot with boiling water, and let it steep for three to five minutes. The general rule is to add 1 tablespoon of fresh herb leaves or flowers for each cup of tea plus a little extra. So the old method of adding "one for thee, one for me, and one for the pot" works quite nicely.

Tea made from the flowers of chamomile is very common in Switzerland. You can usually order it at most bars in France, Italy, and Spain. Mint is widely consumed in the Arab world, usually with the addition of way too much sugar. The best thing to do is to try out a few blends of leaves to find what will suit your fancy.

Mint Julep

Mint julep is not exactly a tea, but it is a beverage and a very popular one in the South, especially around Derby Day. A classic mint julep is made in a metal cup, but any tumbler will do. Place a handful of crushed ice in the tumbler, add three to four leaves of fresh mint and $^1/_2$ teaspoon sugar. Mash all that up with a spoon and pour in one to two ounces of Kentucky bourbon. I remember drinking mint julep from a metal bucket with a group of Missouri men who invited me to join them as they passed the bucket around one sultry August night after broadcasting the fiddler's contest at the Boone County Fair. Heritage and tradition are often rooted in the herb garden.

Week Eighteen (LATE JUNE) *Harvest herbs for cooking.*

Fish on the grill is rapidly becoming a popular substitute for burgers, chicken, and steak. But don't top that fish with tartar sauce unless you've made it with your own fresh tarragon. Or why not spoon a little of the herb sauce in the following recipe over fish for a new taste treat.

Fish with Herb Sauce

4 fish steaks, 1-inch thick, either halibut, cod, or salmon

2 tablespoons each chopped parsley, chervil, chives, sorrel, and tarragon

^{1}/$_3$ cup chopped onion

1 clove garlic, peeled and chopped

^{1}/$_2$ cup olive oil

3 tablespoons white wine vinegar

1 tablespoon Dijon mustard

1. Place all the ingredients except the fish in a blender or food processor and blend to a smooth but still slightly chunky sauce.

2. Prepare the barbecue grill or kitchen broiler and cook the fish steaks for five minutes on each side.

3. Place a fish steak on a plate, spoon some of the sauce over it, and garnish with a few sprigs of fresh herbs.

Serves 4

Week Nineteen (EARLY JULY) *Harvest herbs for potpourri.*

Potpourri is nothing more than a blend of dried herbs and other ingredients that give off a pleasant fragrance. Vendors selling dried herbs at markets are very common in France, Italy, and Spain.

In your herb garden you have grown lavender, bergamot, anise hyssop, chamomile, mint, and rosemary as potpourri herbs. Fragrant rose petals blended with any of these herbs add color and texture to potpourri.

Harvest herbs for potpourri early in the morning after the dew has dried but before the sun gets too hot, which will cause the plants to wilt slightly. When harvesting lavender, use the spikes with the blue flowers only, but when gathering other potpourri herbs, harvest the stems, leaves, and flowers intact. Bring the herbs immediately in out of the sun into the shade. Air circulation is very important, so spread the herbs out on an old window screen or a piece of muslin or cheesecloth that is stretched out over a frame. Place the drying herbs in an attic, garage, barn, or some other shady area with good circulation, not the basement. Herbs should dry in three to four days.

To make the potpourri simply blend together the leaves and flowers you think are attractive and place them in a bowl to allow their fragrance to permeate the room. You can also stuff little pouches of cloth with potpourri, sew them up, and use them to perfume closets or dresser drawers.

Week Twenty (MID-JULY) *Harvest herbs for cooking.*

It is hot and humid in mid-July, and your herbs are really thriving. It is important to keep picking your herbs and cooking with them to keep them from going to flower and using up all their flavor and energy. Hot weather really enhances the flavor of basil and oregano.

Neapolitan Pizza with Fresh Basil and Oregano

Summertime pizza is my favorite to make. You can top the dough with red, ripe tomatoes and flavor them with your own fresh herbs. Tiny piccolo basil is the best for this, but whatever basil you plant will be wonderful. This is the type of pizza that was served to me in old Napoli.

1 pound fresh or frozen pizza dough, enough to make one pie
¹/₂ pound mozzarella cheese
2 large, ripe, fresh tomatoes
2 tablespoons each fresh minced basil and Greek oregano
2 tablespoons extra-virgin or virgin olive oil

1. Preheat the oven to 400 degrees F.

2. Lightly oil the pizza pan and stretch the dough over it.

3. Slice the cheese into thin wafers and spread it over the dough.

4. Peel the tomatoes by cutting out the core and then dropping them into a pan of boiling water for ten seconds. Remove them and let them cool for one minute. The peels will slip right off. Scoop out as much of the seeds and juice as you can and then slice the tomatoes. Layer them over the cheese.

5. Sprinkle the fresh herbs over the tomatoes and sprinkle the olive oil over that.

6. Place the pizza in the oven for fifteen to twenty minutes or until the dough is lightly browned on the bottom.

Variation: To make Pizza Provençal, eliminate the cheese, basil, and oregano and substitute fresh, minced rosemary, black olives, and anchovies.

Week Twenty-one (MID- TO LATE JULY) *Add more mulch; water.*

The heat and usual drought of July will cause your herbs to suffer a little bit, even though you have enriched your soil with organic matter and covered the ground with mulch. You might need to add additional mulch and to water the herb garden.

The best way to water is slowly with a soaker hose. Snake your soaker hose through the garden in an S shape, connect it to your regular hose, and turn on the water halfway. Let the water run for two hours and then probe the soil with a hand trowel to see if the ground is saturated to a depth of at least 4 inches. If the ground is saturated, turn off the hose; if not, continue for another hour or more. Don't water again for at least another week, and then repeat the process. If you get any rain, you may not need to water at all.

Week Twenty-two (LATE JULY) *Replant dill, chervil, and cilantro for fall harvest.*

Usually by late July the dill and cilantro plants in your garden have started flowering and producing seeds, which make the edible leaves more bitter. Now is a good time to pull up these spent plants, get rid of the old, and plant new. Simply dig up their areas in the garden, smooth out the soil, sprinkle on some new seeds, and pat them into the soil. Be sure the seeds are lightly covered. Watering is critical now because you are not likely to get much rain. Use your watering can to water these herbs lightly and daily until they germinate. Then reduce your watering to every other day until they get established at 2 to 3 inches tall. By then the cooler days and nights of September will arrive, and you will have these herbs to eat fresh all the way until a hard winter frost.

Week Twenty-three (EARLY AUGUST) Harvest herbs to cook.

Rosemary and thyme are two herbs that really release their flavors with meats grilled on an outdoor barbecue. You can marinate meat with them and even toss their stems into the fire to give off an additional smoky aroma.

Rosemary and Thyme Grilled Chicken

1 whole chicken, cut up, or 2 to 3 pounds chicken parts
2 tablespoons olive or other vegetable oil
juice of one lemon
¹/₂ cup fresh rosemary and thyme
salt and pepper to taste

1. Remove the leaves from the stems of the rosemary and thyme. Discard the stems but reserve the leaves.

2. Place the chicken pieces in a large pan and sprinkle them with the fresh herbs, oil, lemon juice, salt, and pepper. Cover, place in the refrigerator, and marinate overnight or for at least two hours.

3. Prepare your barbecue grill or kitchen broiler and grill the chicken for fifteen to twenty minutes, basting frequently with any remaining marinade and herbs.

Serves 4

Week Twenty-four (LATE AUGUST) *Harvest other herbs for cooking.*

Cilantro, also known as fresh coriander, is the pungent herbal ingredient in salsa that is always used in Mexico but is seldom seen too far north of the border. If you have always wondered why your homemade salsa just doesn't taste as great as others, the secret is fresh cilantro. It is best to use only the tender leaves and discard the flowers and stems, which are usually too bitter to use.

Cilantro Salsa

2 tablespoons each fresh cilantro and parsley, chopped
2 large, fresh, ripe tomatoes, cored and chopped
1 large green bell pepper, cored and chopped
1 jalapeño pepper, seeded and chopped
1 large clove garlic or $^1/_2$ teaspoon prepared garlic
1 medium red, white, or yellow onion, peeled and chopped
juice of two limes

1. Peel and coarsely chop all the vegetables. Place all the ingredients in a blender or food processor and whir to form a chunky salsa. If your processor is not big enough, whir the ingredients in two batches and then stir it all together in a large bowl.

2. Add the lime juice and stir. At this point you may want to taste the salsa and adjust the seasonings by adding a pinch of sugar, salt, pepper, chili powder, or whatever you like.

3. Serve with tortilla chips or use this as a topping for fish or chicken.

Makes 3 cups

Week Twenty-five (EARLY SEPTEMBER) *Harvest herbs to dry.*

Drying your own fresh herbs to use in the winter is a very satisfying way to preserve the experience of your summer herb garden. Herbs that dry really well, ones that I have had success with and that I think are superior to store-bought dried herbs, include basil, thyme, Greek oregano, sage, and rosemary. Dried chervil, chives, dill, and parsley do not have much flavor in my opinion, big herb companies do a better job of drying tarragon than I do, and sorrel is not used as a dried herb. All the tea and potpourri herbs—anise hyssop, lemon balm, chamomile, wild strawberry, bergamot, and lavender—also dry quite well.

Because you are going to dry larger quantities of these herbs, the method of spreading a few herbs on a screen to dry for potpourri will not be adequate. You still should harvest the herbs in the early morning after the dew has dried and before the heat of the sun warms the day. It is also better to harvest herbs for cooking before they flower, if possible, because flowering drains some of the flavor out of the leaves.

Bundle a handful of herb stems together and tie them with a string at the bottom. Hang these bundles in a warm, dry place for four days or until the leaves feel dry to the touch but are still as green as possible.

Then strip the leaves from the stems, place them in airtight jars, and store them on a shelf or spice rack or in a cabinet. Dried culinary herbs make charming Christmas presents if you find yourself with too many for your own use.

Week Twenty-six (MID-SEPTEMBER TO FIRST FROST) *Get garden ready for winter.*

Your herb garden will prosper and produce fresh herbs until October, November, and even December in some areas. But it is important for you to begin preparing the garden for winter now.

After you have harvested all the herbs you need for drying or if you feel you won't be using any more, prune back the perennial herbs: lavender, thyme, tarragon, chives, Greek oregano, sage, sorrel, anise hyssop, mint, lemon balm, wild strawberry, and bergamot. Then mound some compost or peat moss around their roots. Just before cold weather really arrives, cover the garden with a light blanket of hay, straw, pine needles, or dried leaves to protect it from cold. Pull up the annual plants of dill, chervil, basil, cilantro, nasturtium, and borage and place them in the compost pile. Rosemary can be treated as a perennial in many warmer states, but it won't survive a winter in colder states.

Good luck and enjoy your herb garden.

A Classic American Garden

A Classic American Garden is a very good first garden for the whole family to get involved in. You will be growing a little bit of many time-honored and reliable garden varieties including corn, green beans, carrots, beets, lettuce, radishes, zucchini, cucumbers, tomatoes, green peppers, onions, and cantaloupes. This type of garden is somewhat like the World War II Victory Garden.

No Classic American Garden would be complete without a few flowers, so, in addition to vegetables, this garden will also feature a few classic and easy-to-grow favorites such as marigolds, asters, calendulas, zinnias, and bachelor's buttons.

By following the weekly activity schedule, this garden will start producing radishes and lettuce in the early summer, followed by beans, squash, beets, and carrots, then completed with tomatoes, peppers, cucumbers, and cantaloupes. The flowers will start blooming in midsummer and will continue until frost.

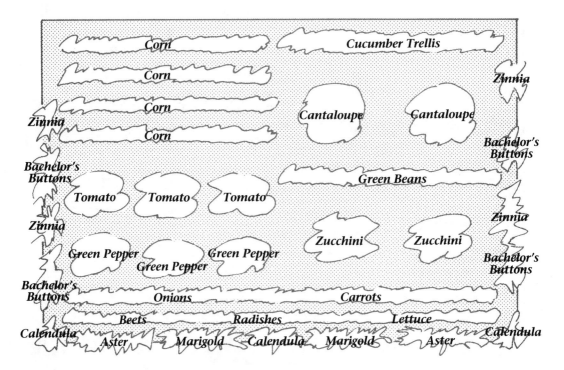

Even though you will be planting corn and cantaloupes, two items that traditionally take up a lot of room in a garden, I have devised a concise planting pattern for the corn and have suggested a space-saving variety of melon to keep this garden a compact 10 feet by 15 feet.

A few of the vegetables are subject to pest attack, but I have included instructions on how you can control these insects with the botanical pesticides pyrethrum and rotenone. You are going to control diseases by enriching the soil and planting disease-resistant varieties.

The seeds and plants for this garden are easy to buy and to plant. Corn, beans, carrots, beets, lettuce, radishes, zucchini, cucumbers, and cantaloupe are some of the easiest plants to grow from seeds planted directly in the garden. You will grow the onions from little bulbs, and you should buy the tomato and pepper plants at your local garden center rather than start them yourself indoors.

Finally, these vegetables are so well known that most people probably know how to cook corn, carrots, and green beans, but I have included seven recipes that I think are a little different and will give you a chance to enjoy your garden produce in a whole new light.

The Weekly Guide

Week One (EARLY FEBRUARY) *Order your seed catalogs.*

It's not absolutely necessary to order seed catalogs for this garden. All the varieties I suggest are readily available at your local garden center, and you can buy your seed packets right off the shelf.

I really like seed catalogs, though, because they are very colorful and fun to read. After a long winter of cabin fever, they can be very inspirational in giving you a lift out of the winter doldrums. Here are a few classic seed catalogs that I think you will enjoy:

- Gurney's Seed & Nursery Co., 110 Capital Street, Yankton, SD 57079; (605) 665–1930. "Home of Hardy Northern Grown Planting Stock," "Helping Gardeners Grow for 126 Years."

- Harris Seeds, 60 Saginaw Drive, Rochester, NY 14692–2960; (716) 442–0410. In business since 1879.
- Henry Field's Seed & Nursery Co., 414 North Burnett, Shenandoah, IA 51602; (605) 665–9391. Field's celebrated its one-hundredth anniversary in 1992.
- J. W. Jung Seed & Nursery Co., 335 High Street, Randolph, WI 53957; (414) 326–3123. Family owned and operated since 1907.
- Park Seed Co., Cokesbury Road, Greenwood, SC 29647; (803) 223–7333. The Park family still runs this firm started in 1868.
- R. H. Shumway's, P.O. Box 1, Graniteville, SC 29829; (803) 663–9771. "Good Seeds Cheap" is their motto.

Week Two (LATE FEBRUARY) *Survey your friends and family.*

While you are waiting for the seed catalogs to arrive, ask your family and friends if they have any favorite vegetables that they really want you to grow. I will give you my suggestions about what you should grow, but there may be a certain type of corn or carrot from their childhood that they want to put in the garden.

Week Three (EARLY MARCH) *Choose your seeds; place your order.*

Buy one packet each of the following seeds:
- Bush beans: either Tendergreen, Blue Lake, Derby, or Top Crop
- Beets: either Detroit Dark Red, Early Wonder, or Red Ace
- Cantaloupe: either Musketeer or Midget Bush
- Carrots: either Royal Chantenay, Nantes, or Danvers
- Corn: either Seneca for yellow kernels or Silver Queen for white
- Cucumber: either Marketmore, Burpee's Hybrid, or Sweet Success
- Lettuce: either Black-Seeded Simpson, Red Sails, or Oak Leaf
- Radish: either Cherry Belle, Champion, or Sparkler
- Zucchini: either Black, Grey, or Aristocrat
- Asters: dwarf variety, mixed colors
- Bachelor's buttons: all blue or mixed red, white, and blue
- Calendula: dwarf variety, mixed colors

- Marigolds: small 10- to 12-inch types, any color
- Zinnia: dwarf variety, mixed colors
- Onions: either one quart of sets or one bunch of onion plants such as Granex Hybrid, Walla Walla, Texas Sweet, or Red Wethersfield, the classic hamburger onion

Remember that you will buy your tomato and pepper plants at a garden center, your cucumbers will grow on a trellis, and the vines of your cantaloupes will be short and compact rather than long and spreading.

Week Four (MID-MARCH) *Choose your garden site; buy fertilizer.*

The Classic American Garden needs to be 10 feet wide, or deep, and 15 feet long. Please refer to the diagram at the beginning of this chapter. You need to find an appropriate place in your yard to accommodate this type of garden. It needs full sun; that is, the garden site needs to be bathed in full sun, no shade, for at least six full hours each day. Eight hours is preferable. The area needs to be level and well drained; no water should be left standing, making the ground soggy, a day after a heavy rain. Find an appropriate site in your yard and mark it off with stakes. Clear the area of any rocks, leaves, sticks, and debris.

Go to the hardware store or garden center and buy a 2- to 5-pound box of balanced natural organic fertilizer. Look for ingredients such as hydrolyzed feather meal, wheat germ, soybean meal, bone meal, and composted manure. If you can't find what you want, ask for it.

While you are shopping, you might as well buy the supplies you will need to build the cucumber trellis: three 5- to 6-foot long wooden or metal stakes and a piece of wire or metal mesh fence 6 feet in length. Also, buy a 4-cubic-foot bag of sphagnum peat moss and four 40-pound bags of compost or composted manure. You are going to add these to the garden to improve the soil next week.

Week Five (LATE MARCH) *Prepare the garden for planting.*

Remove any grass or sod from the top of your garden space. Either dig up the area by hand or till it with a rotary tiller. You might have to go over the area a couple of times, especially if it's a new garden site. You can rent a Rototiller or hire someone to do it for you. Be sure to break up all the clumps.

Read the package instructions and spread the appropriate amount of fertilizer over the garden, usually 1 to 2 pounds. Spread a 2- to 4-inch layer of organic matter—either peat moss, compost, or shredded leaves—over the garden and dig or till these materials into the soil. Use all the peat moss and compost you bought last week. Rake the garden smooth and you are ready to plant.

Week Six (LATE MARCH TO EARLY APRIL) *Plant lettuce, carrots, radishes, beets, and onions.*

Please refer to the planting diagram at the beginning of this chapter. You will see that this garden has narrower rows and is more tightly spaced than the usual garden. This is the "backyard intensive" method of gardening. Wide-row gardens are designed so that tractors with mechanical cultivators can run up and down the rows. I don't think your backyard will accommodate a large tractor. Vegetables can be planted this closely because you have enriched your soil so well with organic fertilizer and organic matter that everything will grow splendidly.

For the beets, radishes, and lettuce, stretch your row marker over the entire 15-foot length across the front of the garden. Dig a $1/2$-inch-deep trench under the row marker and sprinkle the beet seeds for 5 feet, the radish seeds for 5 feet, and the lettuce seeds for 5 feet. Lightly cover with soil and firm down with your hand. Water.

For the onions and carrots, move back a foot and stretch the row marker again. Plant half the row in onions and half in carrots. For onion sets poke a hole in the ground with your finger just 1 inch deep. Place the onion in the hole and cover with soil. Tamp the soil with your hand. For onion plants dig a 1-inch deep hole, place the onion in it, and firm the soil around the plant.

For carrots try to find a 1- to 2-pound can of ordinary sand from a fresh-water beach or a sandbox. Carrots love sandy soil, and it really helps them grow straight if you add sand to the garden. Dig the sand into the area where you plan to plant the carrots and dig a trench $1/2$ inch deep. Sprinkle in the carrot seeds, cover with soil, and firm down. Water.

Remember to keep the seeds watered with a watering can almost every day until they germinate in a week to ten days.

Week Seven (MID-APRIL) *Buy tomatoes and peppers.*

You are only going to have room in this garden for three tomato plants and three pepper plants. Choose three of the same of each or a combination of red, orange, plum, or cherry tomatoes, and hot and sweet peppers. There are dozens of tomato and pepper varieties; just ask your garden center what grows well in your area and pick out what interests you. Remember to keep your tomato and pepper plants watered and protected from harsh wind and frost until you plant them.

Week Eight (MID-APRIL) *Build a cucumber trellis.*

Cucumbers grow on long trailing vines that grow better if they can climb up off the ground and onto a trellis. A trellis also maximizes your garden space and makes picking the cucumbers easier. Your trellis will be approximately 6 feet long and 3 to 4 feet high.

Sink the posts into the soil at the back of the garden according to the garden diagram at the beginning of this chapter, one at either end and one in the middle, and pound them in with a hammer or other heavy object. Stretch the fencing along the posts and attach it with wire or string.

Week Nine (LATE APRIL TO EARLY MAY) *Harvest radishes; thin radishes, lettuce, and beets.*

It may be a little early yet, but some of your radishes may be large enough to pick. It is a good idea to thin out the rows of radishes, lettuce, and beets now to give the remaining ones room to fill out. Here's how.

Pull up any radishes that look large enough to eat. Then carefully pull up radish sprouts, leaving the remaining radishes spaced 1 inch apart in the row.

Thin the lettuce row by pulling up any lettuce sprouts, leaving 3 inches between sprouts in the row.

Thin the beets by pulling up enough sprouts to leave 2 inches between sprouts in the row.

All these thinnings make a great addition to a salad.

Week Ten (MID-MAY) *Plant tomatoes and peppers.*

Please refer to the planting diagram at the beginning of this chapter. Plant the peppers and tomatoes in the middle of the garden on the left side. Set each plant in the exact place where you are going to plant it. Take a second look and be sure the plants are spaced approximately 2 feet apart in the row.

Now use your trowel to dig a hole that is at least twice the size of the tomato root ball. Break up any dirt balls and remove any rocks from the hole.

Sprinkle in 1 tablespoon of natural organic fertilizer into the hole, remove the tomato from the pot, and place it in the hole. Firm the soil up around the plant, pat it down with your hands, and water. Repeat with the remaining tomatoes and plant the peppers in exactly the same way.

Tomato and pepper plants can easily be killed by late spring frosts, which are still common at this time of year in many parts of the country. If the weatherman predicts a killing frost, protect your plants by covering them at night with paper or plastic "hot caps" available at garden centers or with inverted baskets or pots or even with a light cloth propped up with sticks like a circus tent so it doesn't crush the plants.

Week Eleven (MID- TO LATE MAY) *Plant corn, cucumbers, cantaloupes, zucchini, and beans.*

Plant the corn in a grid pattern, 12 inches apart in each direction, four rows deep. Simply mark an area 4 feet wide and 7 feet long. Mark a row 7 feet long across the back of the garden. Place the corn kernels 12 inches apart in the row and 2 inches deep. Cover the seeds with soil and firm down. Mark another row 12 inches away from the first one and repeat until you have planted four rows.

Plant the cucumbers by digging a $^1/_2$-inch-deep trench on either side of the base of your cucumber trellis. Place the seeds 4 inches apart, cover with soil, and firm down.

Plant the cantaloupes in two circles, also called hills, spaced 2 feet from the cucumber trellis and 3 feet apart from one another. Draw two circles in the soil, each 18 inches in diameter. Arrange six seeds over the area of each circle and plant the seeds by poking them into the soil 1 inch deep. Cover with soil and firm down.

Plant the green beans in a row, 2 feet away from the cucumber circles. Dig a trench 1 inch deep, plant the bean seeds 4 inches apart in the row, cover with soil, and firm down.

Plant the zucchini in two circles, exactly the same as the cantaloupe circles, 2 feet away from the green bean row. The zucchini plants have to grow between the beans and the carrots.

Water all the seeds you have planted today. Be sure to water the seeds you have planted previously. Keep all seeds watered until they germinate.

Week Twelve (LATE MAY) *Plant flowers; make first big spring salad.*

The idea with these flowers is just to tuck a few blossoms in here and there to give the garden splashes of color. Plant them all in shallow trenches, no more than ¹/₂ inch deep, lightly cover with soil, and firm down. Water. The calendulas, asters, and marigolds are all approximately the same height, so intersperse them along the front and corners of the garden. The zinnias and bachelor's buttons are the same height, 2 to 2¹/₂ feet tall, so intersperse them along the sides of the garden.

Spring Garden Tossed Salad

Now is a good time to enjoy a salad of tender lettuce, shredded sweet carrots and beets, and a few slices of young onions.

> *2 heads leaf lettuce (about 4 cups)*
> *2 to 3 medium-sized beets*
> *2 to 3 medium carrots*
> *2 to 3 onions*
> *10 to 12 radishes*
> *3 tablespoons olive or other salad oil*
> *1 tablespoon red wine vinegar*
> *salt and pepper to taste*

1. Wash and separate the lettuce leaves. Dry and place in a large salad bowl.

2. Wash and trim the tops off the beets. Simmer beets in a pan of water for fifteen minutes or until tender. Drain, peel, and shred.

3. Wash and trim the tops off the carrots. Simmer carrots in a pan of water for fifteen minutes. Drain and shred. Toss the beets and the carrots over the lettuce.

4. Peel and trim the onions and slice. Trim and slice the radishes. Toss over the salad.

5. Pour the olive oil and vinegar over the salad and sprinkle with salt and pepper to taste. (You can use your own salad dressing if you prefer.) Toss the whole salad and serve.

Serves 4

Week Thirteen (EARLY JUNE) *Pull weeds; install soaker hose; mulch.*

Now is the time to cage your tomatoes. Buy three tomato cages at your garden center and place them over your tomato plants, forcing the stakes down into the ground. The tomatoes will grow up in these cages, making it easier to pick them. Buy the heavy-duty cages because they last longer and are a better investment. You won't need to cage your pepper plants.

You may have a few weeds popping up in the garden. The best time to pull weeds is after a rain when the ground is soft and wet. You don't have to pull all the weeds in the garden because you are going to put down mulch. Just pull the big ones and any that are crowding your plants in their rows. Cultivation of the rows by pulling weeds helps the rain penetrate the soil and aerates the soil, bringing oxygen to the microorganisms and worms, which are busy making your garden soil rich and fertile.

The best way to water your garden is with a soaker hose. It is more effective and conserves water better than any other method of irrigation. Simply snake your 50-foot hose through the plants in the garden in an S pattern. A soaker will drench the ground 18 inches on either side of the hose, so one hose should be adequate. Leave this hose in place in the garden for the rest of the season and then attach a regular hose to it to water the garden later in the season.

Place a 6-inch layer of straw or hay mulch on top of the soaker hose and between the rows, around the tomato and pepper plants, at the base of the trellis, and around the circles of cantaloupes and zucchini. Get as close as you can without covering the plants. The mulch will smother the weeds and conserve water.

Week Fourteen (MID-JUNE) *Harvest beets; continue thinning lettuce and radishes.*

Everything in your garden should be up and growing by now. Be sure to pull any persistent weeds and rearrange the mulch if the wind has blown it around. Keep thinning and eating the lettuce and radishes. As soon as your beets are the size of golf balls or larger, harvest by pulling them from the ground and shaking off the soil. Now you are ready to make a cool and creamy cold beet borscht.

Creamy Beet Borscht

3 to 4 medium-sized beets
2 cups buttermilk or milk
2 cups sour cream or yogurt
salt and pepper to taste
2 onions from the garden

1. Wash the beets and trim off the tops and stems. Place in a pan of water and simmer over medium heat thirty minutes or until tender. Drain and peel.

2. Chop the beets and place them in a food processor. Add the buttermilk or milk and sour cream or yogurt. Process to a smooth soup. Add salt and pepper to taste.

3. Place the soup in a container and refrigerate for two hours. Taste for seasonings. At this point you may want to add a tablespoon of fresh dill or parsley for flavor.

4. Trim the roots off the onions and slice them very thin. Ladle soup into bowls and sprinkle with the onion slices.

Serves 4

Week Fifteen (LATE JUNE) *Be on pest patrol.*

Now is the time that insect pests start making their way into your garden. By adding organic matter and natural fertilizer to your garden, you have done everything you can to give your plants a fighting chance. You may not have any pest infestations at all, but you should examine your plants at least once a week to see if any bugs are there. If you are ever in doubt, capture one of the bugs in a jar and take it to your cooperative extension office or garden center for identification. Here's what to look for:

- Beans: Look for the Mexican bean beetle, which is $1/2$-inch long and has a yellow-brown shell with black spots. Don't mistake it for a ladybug, which has an orange-red shell. Control with pyrethrum or rotenone spray or powder.

- Cucumbers and Cantaloupes: Look for cucumber beetles, $1/2$-inch long and greenish-yellow with a black head. Treat with pyrethrum or rotenone powder or spray.

- Corn: Look for corn borers, 1-inch-long grayish-pink caterpillars. Control with pyrethrum.
- Tomatoes: Look for tomato hornworms, 1-inch-long pale green caterpillars. Control with *Bt*.
- Zucchini: Look for squash vine borers, striped cucumber beetles, and squash bugs. Control with pyrethrum or rotenone spray or powder.

Week Sixteen (LATE JUNE) *Harvest carrots.*

Keep an eye out for bugs, pull any errant weeds, and keep harvesting lettuce, radishes, and beets. As soon as carrots are the size of your little finger or larger, harvest what you need by pulling them from the ground; leave the rest behind till next time. Now is the time to enjoy one of the world's best tasting foods, a young carrot straight from the garden.

Braised Carrots
in Creamy Herb Sauce

1 pound carrots, washed, trimmed, and sliced thin

1 tablespoon each unsalted butter and olive oil

¹/₂ teaspoon dried or 2 sprigs fresh tarragon

¹/₂ cup chicken stock or water

1 teaspoon French coarse-grained country mustard

³/₄ cup sour cream or low-fat yogurt

2 tablespoons minced fresh parsley

salt and pepper to taste

1. In a heavy skillet melt the butter and olive oil over medium heat. Add the carrots and sauté for two minutes.

2. Add the tarragon and stock and cover. Simmer for three to five minutes.

3. In a separate bowl mix the mustard and the parsley with the sour

cream or yogurt. Add to the carrots. Cook the carrots and cream sauce over low heat for two minutes. Do not boil. Season with salt and pepper to taste and serve.

Serves 4

Week Seventeen (EARLY JULY) *Fertilize garden.*

At this point in the garden season, the beans, cucumbers, tomatoes, peppers, zucchini, and cantaloupes are beginning to blossom. Now is a very important time to add extra fertilizer because the plants have used up a great portion of the fertilizer you applied earlier in the season.

Simply sprinkle a tablespoon of natural organic fertilizer around the base of each tomato and pepper plant, 2 tablespoons per circle of cucumbers and zucchini, and $^1/_2$ cup per row of beans, corn, and cucumbers. The rest of the vegetables and flowers don't need any extra fertilizer.

Week Eighteen (MID-JULY) *Watch for bugs; water.*

Continue to examine your plants for insects. You may notice the presence of ladybugs and praying mantises, as well as birds and toads. Welcome them to your garden because they all eat enormous numbers of insects that might otherwise attack your garden.

Unless you have gotten a lot of rain recently, your garden can probably use watering about now. Simply attach a garden hose from your spigot to your buried soaker hose. Turn on the water and let it run for at least two hours. The water will slowly drip out and saturate the ground. Turn off the water and don't water again for at least another week.

Week Nineteen (MID- TO LATE JULY) *Harvest cucumbers, green beans, and zucchini.*

Depending on the weather, you should be ready to begin harvesting some of the classic summer vegetables that form the mainstay of your garden. Cucumbers from the garden have a more pronounced flavor than the store-bought variety, but they should be picked while they are still young so they don't have a chance to get bitter. Pick beans and zucchini when they are young and tender, too, when they taste the sweetest.

Swedish Cucumber Salad

This salad is so refreshing, it helps cool off the warmest summer day.

2 large cucumbers
1 pint sour cream
2 tablespoons minced fresh dill
1 small clove garlic, peeled and minced
salt and pepper to taste

1. Peel the cucumbers and cut them lengthwise into quarters. Remove the seeds and slice the cucumbers thinly. Place in a medium mixing bowl.

2. Spoon the sour cream over the cucumbers, sprinkle with half of the dill, the garlic, and salt and pepper to taste. Stir to blend well.

3. Spoon the cucumber salad into a mixing bowl and garnish with the remaining minced dill.

Serves 4

Week Twenty (EARLY AUGUST) *Succotash time.*

Succotash is probably the most classic of all classic garden dishes. The creamy mixture of fresh sweet corn and green beans is always a summer favorite.

Sweet corn is ready to eat when the tassels turn brown. Each stalk should have one to two ears of corn. Simply pull the ears away from the stalk and tear off the husks and silks.

In many parts of the country, even the most densely populated urban and suburban areas, raccoons, deer, and birds will discover you are growing corn, zero in on your crop, and devour it. The only reliable way to stop raccoons and deer is to build a sturdy electric fence around your garden. The only way to deter birds is to drape a lightweight fabric netting over the corn as soon as the ears begin to form. Leave the netting there until you have harvested your corn. Both electric fences and fabric netting are available at garden centers.

Pick the green beans when they are still young and tender. Don't wait for them to get large and tough. Harvest the zucchini when they are less than 5 inches long (at this size they don't have any seeds); slice them off the vine with a sharp knife.

Fresh Garden Succotash

Many purists say that true succotash is made with lima or shell beans. But this recipe uses green beans and adds peppers, onions and zucchini to take full advantage of your own fresh garden produce. Serve as a side dish to steak or chicken on the barbecue.

> *2 tablespoons butter or oil*
> *1 medium onion, peeled and chopped, enough to make 1 cup*
> *2 cups green beans*
> *1 medium green bell pepper*
> *4 ears sweet corn*
> *2 small zucchini*
> *1 tablespoon all-purpose flour*
> *1 cup milk*
> *salt and pepper to taste*

1. Melt the butter in a large pan over medium-low heat. Add the onion and fry gently for five minutes.

2. Trim the green beans and cut them into 1-inch pieces. Add to the pan and sauté.

3. Core and chop the green pepper, cut the corn kernels off the cob with a sharp knife, and slice the zucchini into thin slices. Add all of this to the pan and sauté for five minutes, stirring often.

4. Sprinkle the flour over the vegetables and stir to blend well. Add the milk and stir to form a creamy sauce. Add the salt and pepper, keep the heat on low, and simmer for ten minutes.

Serves 4

Week Twenty-one (MID-AUGUST) *Tomatoes are here.*

Tomatoes are the number one favorite of all garden plants to grow. They are best eaten plain in salads or stuffed with cottage cheese or shrimp salad or made into fresh tomato soup.

Fried Green Tomatoes

Sometimes it seems that your tomatoes just won't ever get ripe. For those of you who just can't wait for the tomatoes to fully ripen, here's a recipe for fried green tomatoes.

4 large green or firm pink tomatoes
1/4 cup flour
1 tablespoon sugar
1 1/2 teaspoon salt
1/8 teaspoon ground black pepper
2 cups vegetable oil for frying

1. Cut the tomatoes into 1/2-inch thick slices.

2. Combine flour, sugar, salt, and pepper in a mixing bowl. Lightly coat the tomatoes in the flour mixture.

3. Heat the oil in a heavy frying pan or deep-sided skillet and fry the tomatoes until golden brown.

Serves 4 (as an appetizer)

Week Twenty-two (LATE AUGUST) *Replant lettuce, beets, and radishes; weed; water.*

Pull up and discard any lettuce or radishes left in their rows. Pull up any beets still in the ground and put them in the refrigerator, where they will keep for a couple of weeks. Dig up the rows with a forked spade and smooth with a rake. Replant the lettuce, radishes, and beets, keep them watered, and you will get a second crop that will last up till the first hard frost in the fall.

Keep weeds under control with more mulch and be sure to water the garden with the soaker hose no more than once a week.

Week Twenty-three (LABOR DAY) *Enjoy a beautiful cut-flower bouquet.*

Even though bachelor's buttons, zinnias, calendulas, asters, and marigolds are some of the most common and old-fashioned flowers you can grow, they make a beautiful summer bouquet vivid with color. Simply pick out an appropriate vase, remembering that marigolds, asters, and calendulas have rather short stems; then pick the flowers, cutting the stem length to match the vase. Don't worry about the length when picking; you can always trim the stems to size when you get indoors. Of course you can make two bouquets; a tall bouquet of bachelor's buttons and zinnias and a shorter bouquet of calendulas and asters.

Cut the flowers early in the morning before the heat of the day causes them to wilt. You should cut the stems at a 45-degree angle using a sharp knife, but if that is not possible, at least cut them cleanly and evenly. Bring them indoors or into the shade immediately and place them in a pail of water while you arrange them in the vase. Fill the vase with cold water and place the bouquet out where everyone can see it.

Week Twenty-four (MID-SEPTEMBER) *Keep up with the harvest.*

Some parts of the country may have already been hit with a light frost announcing the advent of winter and the end of the garden season, whereas some parts are still hot. School has started again, vacations are over, and people are getting busy with other projects.

Keep harvesting your garden and, if you haven't eaten all of your cantaloupes, try making this refreshing dessert.

Cantaloupe Sorbet

1 cantaloupe

6 tablespoons heavy cream

2 teaspoons fresh orange juice

3 teaspoons fresh lime juice

3 tablespoons sugar or honey

1. Harvest cantaloupe when the fruit slips easily off the vine. It should be firm to the touch but give a little, and you should be able to smell the fruit inside. Peel and seed the melon and cut the flesh into 1-inch chunks.

2. Place the melon chunks in a blender or food processor. Add cream, orange and lime juices, and sugar or honey and puree the mixture.

3. Put the mixture in a flat metal pan and place it in the freezer. Stir the melon mixture every fifteen minutes to ensure an even texture and freeze for about one hour.

Makes about $1^1/_2$ pints

Week Twenty-five (LATE SEPTEMBER) *Keep harvesting.*

If it is still warm where you are, this is the time of year when your green peppers become fully ripe and start to turn red. Add the peppers to your scrambled eggs or grill them on the barbecue. Your new lettuce should be coming in, along with the radishes and some tiny young beets. Keep harvesting and enjoying your garden.

Week Twenty-six (FALL) *Start putting the garden to bed.*

As cold weather sets in, at least cooler nights, it is important to start getting your garden ready for winter. Pull up the spent corn stalks, bean plants, vines, everything. Shred them and put them in the compost pile. If you have any leftover compost or mulch, spread it over the garden now. When the leaves come down, shred them with your lawn mower or shredder and spread them over the garden like a blanket. You can till all of this organic matter into the garden now or wait till spring to do it. Either way, your garden will be ready to start again come next spring.

A Gourmet
Culinary Garden

A *Gourmet Culinary Garden is a garden for people who have traveled in Europe and remember the special flavors of all the interesting and tasty fruits and vegetables that they enjoyed over there. It is also a garden for people who have eaten often in French and Italian restaurants and have come to love the fruits and vegetables served there. With the growth of seed catalogs in recent years that specialize in offering international gourmet vegetables, people who love to cook and garden can grow these continental varieties right in their own backyard.*

Instead of growing ordinary garden peas, you will grow tiny petits pois; instead of green beans, you will grow slender haricots verts. The list goes on to include Genovese basil, French tarragon, Mediterranean tomatoes, cornichon cucumbers, red-tinged lettuce, mesclun cutting salad greens, white Italian eggplant, orange Dutch peppers, Charentais melons, and more.

Petits Pois	*Cucumbers*
Radishes	*Tomato* *Green Pepper* *Eggplant*
Lettuce	*Basil* *Basil* *Basil* *Basil*
Carrots	*Tomato* *Green Pepper* *Eggplant*
Beets	*Basil* *Basil*
Arugula	*Haricots Verts*
Mesclun Salad Mix	*Melon* *Melon*
French Tarragon	

This is the garden to grow for people who really love to cook. I have written three cookbooks and dozens of food articles for national and local newspapers. I discovered that all these varieties were available in 1985 when I wrote about gourmet gardening for *USA Today.* Growing these foods rejuvenated my love of gardening and gave me a whole new purpose for my garden each spring ever since. I always try to grow one new gourmet vegetable each year.

This garden begins during the bleak days of winter when you start eggplant, pepper, and tomato plants indoors in your own little windowsill greenhouse. As the seasons warm, you will plant the remaining fruits and vegetables outdoors in a garden that measures no more than 10 feet wide by 15 feet long.

Before you do anything, please read the first three chapters in this book for advice on what tools you will need to buy, how to dig and fertilize your garden, and how to control pests using environmentally friendly methods. I also suggest you read through this entire chapter to get a grip on the work schedule before you begin. The work schedule I outline is flexible. You should take advantage of good weather and the availability of your own precious time to garden when conditions are favorable. Please, adjust my schedule to fit your own.

The Weekly Guide

Week One (LATE JANUARY) Order your seed catalogs.

Simply make a telephone call or send a self-addressed stamped envelope to any or all of the following seed-catalog companies. Besides offering most of the seeds suggested for this garden, these catalogs contain great gardening, and sometimes cooking, information. All these catalog companies pride themselves on offering only the most flavorsome fruits and vegetables. Here are some of my favorite catalogs; go ahead and order all of them.

- The Cook's Garden, P.O. Box 535, Londonderry, VT 05148; (802) 824–3400. This catalog specializes in lettuce and salad greens and offers more than fifty varieties. The owner, Shep Ogden, is a dedicated gardener whose grandfather helped found the organic-gardening movement more than fifty years ago.

- Johnny's Selected Seeds, Foss Hill Road, Albion, ME 04910–9731; (207) 437–4301. Johnny's has a very good selection of gourmet seeds tucked in with the rest of the seed offerings. A very informative catalog full of specific gardening tips and techniques.
- Nichols Garden Nursery, 1190 North Pacific Highway, Albany, OR 97321–4598; (503) 928–9280. A great West Coast source of gourmet and international seeds at very reasonable prices.
- Shepherd's Garden Seeds, 30 Irene Street, Torrington, CT 06790; (203) 482–3638; West Coast gardeners can call (408) 335–6910. Renee Shepherd scours European markets and gardens each year looking for only the best varieties.
- Thompson & Morgan, P.O. Box 1308, Jackson, NJ 08527; (908) 363–2225. This is the prestigious British seed house that once provided seeds for Darwin's experiments and to many of the crowned heads of Europe.

Week Two (EARLY FEBRUARY) *Survey your friends and family.*

A lot of people have taste memories of a luscious melon they once ate in Paris or a sprightly arugula salad they ate in Rome. Ask your friends and family if they have any special garden items they want you to plant; then make a list. I am giving you a list of what I think you should plant, but you might want to make a few variations.

Week Three (MID-FEBRUARY) *Place your seed order.*

Now is the time to place your order. Your seed catalogs should have arrived, and you are probably as enthusiastic as I am this time of year when trying to decide which seeds to buy.

I will give you instructions on how to start your own pepper, tomato, eggplant, and basil plants indoors. If you wish, you can buy plants already started for you at a garden center, although seed starting is a lot of fun and really quite easy. I suggest that you buy one packet each of the following seeds.

- Petits pois: Precovil, Petit Provençal, Waverex, or Argona; tiny peas in slender pods
- Lettuce: Merveilles des Quatres Saisons, Tom Thumb, Rouge d'Hiver, Lollo Rossa, or Romaine
- Radish: D'Avignon, Easter Egg, or French Breakfast
- Mesclun salad mix: Misticanza, Niçoise, Piquant, or Napa Valley; usually a blended mixture of several varieties of lettuces, chicories, herbs, and other salad greens. You cut it, and it grows back.
- Arugula (also called Roquette or Rocket): tangy salad green that looks like dandelion leaves
- Beets: Chioggia is a red beet with white rings inside.
- Carrots: Minicor, Planet, Kundulus, or Thumbelina; all tiny baby carrots
- Haricots verts: Triumph de Farcy, Radar, or Verandon
- Melon: Charentais, Galia, Chaca, or Charmel
- Cornichon: Verte de Massy, Cornichon, or De Bourbonne. These cukes are grown to be picked when they are the size of your thumb, but they are also quite nice when they get slightly larger.
- Eggplant: Osterei, Rosa Bianca for a white eggplant, or Pirouette or Prelane for tiny purple eggplants. Flavor is the same and they cook up the same; you make the choice.
- Tomato: Marmande, Dona, Lorissa, or Costoluto Genovese. All these tomatoes are suggested for their rich tomato taste, but they are also good producers and resistant to diseases.
- Golden peppers: Quadrato D'Oro, Corona, or Orobelle; just like sweet green bell peppers only yellow.
- Genovese basil (also called perfume basil): This large-leafed basil variety is by far the most aromatic and flavorful.

Remember that many local garden centers offer a wide variety of gourmet fruits and vegetable plants that are already started for you. They may very well have tomato, eggplant, basil, and pepper plants that you can buy and thus save yourself the extra work of starting your own seeds indoors. In any event you will need to buy one pot of French tarragon at a garden center because tarragon just does not grow well from seed.

Week Four (LATE FEBRUARY) *Choose your garden site.*

Even though it might still be chilly outdoors, find a spot for your garden that measures 10 feet by 15 feet, that is not shaded by trees or shrubs, and that does not become soggy or waterlogged during the rainy seasons. Your garden needs to be bathed in at least six, preferably eight, hours of pure sunshine every day to thrive. Also, find a place that is not too far from the house so that you can easily get water to it when you need to. Clear the area now, removing any rocks, furniture, and debris.

Week Five (LATE FEBRUARY TO EARLY MARCH) *Buy seed-starting supplies at your garden center.*

If you have decided to start your own tomato, pepper, eggplant, and basil seedlings indoors, go to a garden center and buy your supplies now. Be sure to ask the garden center to order a pot of French, not the tasteless Russian, tarragon for you.

Buy twenty-four small peat pots, one small bag of potting soil, and a plastic "mini-greenhouse." I suggest that you start six plants each of tomato, pepper, eggplant, and basil. You won't plant all of these, but at least you will be protected if a couple of plants die. You can always give away the extra plants you have grown. While you are at your garden center, you might as well buy big bags of compost, peat, and fertilizer. Buy one 4-cubic-foot bag of sphagnum peat moss, four 40-pound bags of compost or composted manure, and a 5- to 10-pound bag of natural organic fertilizer. A truckload of barn sweepings from a local farmer is a great source of fertilizer and organic matter if it is available.

Please read the information on soil, mulch, and fertilizer that is given in the chapter Setting Up the Garden. You might also ask if the garden center has straw, mulched hay, or other mulch. You will need to buy four bales of straw or hay to mulch your garden. You can buy it now or wait until later in the spring if you don't want the bales loitering in your backyard.

Also, buy the supplies you will need to build a pea fence and cucumber trellis. Buy six 5-foot-long wooden or metal stakes and two lengths of fencing wire or stout nylon fencing mesh, 7 feet long and 3 to 4 feet high.

Read the chapter on garden tools in this book and buy whatever tools you need that you don't already have. It is better to have your own than to borrow.

Week Six (EARLY MARCH) *Start peppers, tomatoes, and eggplants indoors.*

Start your seedlings by first filling the peat pots with potting soil about four-fifths full. Tamp the soil down lightly. Sprinkle three to four seeds of one variety in each pot. Fill six pots with tomato seeds, six with pepper seeds, six with eggplant seeds, and six with basil seeds. Sprinkle a half teaspoon of potting soil over the seeds and firm down lightly. Carefully spoon one tablespoon of tepid tap water on top of each pot and place the pots in the mini-greenhouse. Place the top on the mini-greenhouse and put it in a warm sunny location.

Week Seven (MID-MARCH) *Keep the seedlings watered and warm.*

Check the mini-greenhouse and your seed pots every day. Keep them warm and lightly watered but not soaked. In a week to ten days, the seedlings should appear.

Week Eight (MID-MARCH) *Thin seedlings; separate.*

When the seedlings are approximately an inch tall and have their second set of leaves, you need to remove all but one of the seedlings from the pot. This will allow the remaining one to grow strong and tall. Remove the redundant seedlings by snipping them off at the soil level with a very sharp knife or pair of scissors. Discard the seedlings.

Week Nine (MID- TO LATE MARCH) *Prepare the garden soil.*

You need to start preparing the garden soil for planting as soon as the ground is no longer frozen and soggy. Strip off any grass or sod growing in your garden space. Dig the soil to a depth of 8 inches with a forked spade, making sure you turn the soil and break up any clumps. This is very good exercise, but you could also rent a rotary tiller or hire a person to do the rototilling for you. Look in the Yellow Pages or ask for leads at your garden center.

Open the bags of peat moss and compost or composted manure and spread the entire contents evenly over the garden. Following the package instructions, broadcast 3 to 5 pounds of natural organic fertilizer over the garden. Dig or till the garden again, working all the organic matter and fertilizer deep into the soil. Rake the garden smooth, and you are ready to plant.

Week Ten (EARLY APRIL) *Plant peas, lettuce, and radishes.*

Peas love to grow in cool spring weather and many people like to plant peas on March 17, St. Patrick's Day. I prefer to plant peas on my birthday, April Fool's Day. Plant your peas somewhere near these dates.

Petits pois peas grow in pods on vines 18 to 30 inches long, and they grow best when climbing on a pea fence. To build a pea fence, you will need three 5-foot long wooden or metal stakes and a piece of wire or nylon mesh fence 7 feet long and 3 to 4 feet high. Please look at the garden diagram at the beginning of this chapter. Drive three stakes into the ground, one at either end and one in the middle of a 7-foot span across the back of the garden. String the fence along the stakes and secure it with wire or string.

Dig a 1-inch deep trench along either side of the base of the fence. Plant the peas 4 inches apart on either side of the fence, cover with soil, and firm down. Water.

Move 1 foot away from the pea fence and mark a 7-foot-long row. Dig a trench $^1/_2$ inch deep and plant half that row with radish seeds spaced $^1/_2$ inch apart. Cover with soil, firm down, and water. You will plant the remaining half of that row in two weeks so that all your radishes won't ripen at the same time.

Move another foot away from the radishes and mark a row 7 feet long. Dig a trench $^1/_2$ inch deep and plant lettuce seeds $^1/_2$ inch apart in half the row. Again, you will plant the rest of the row later. Cover with soil, firm down, and water.

Keep the seeds moist but not soggy until they germinate in a week to ten days. Rain may do this work for you, but use your watering can every other day if necessary.

Week Eleven (MID-APRIL) *Plant carrots, beets, mesclun, and arugula.*

Move a foot away from the row of lettuce you planted and mark a row 7 feet long. Dig a trench $^1/_4$ to $^1/_2$ inch deep and sprinkle in the carrot seeds. Cover with soil, firm down, and water.

Move another foot away from the carrots and mark another 7-foot row. Dig a trench $^1/_2$ inch deep and sprinkle in the beet seeds, spaced 1 inch apart. Cover, firm, and water.

Mark another 7-foot row 1 foot away from the beet row. Dig a trench $^1/_4$ inch deep and plant half the arugula seeds. Cover, firm, and water.

Move 18 inches away from the arugula row and mark another 7-foot row. Dig a trench $^1/_4$ to $^1/_2$ inch deep and plant half the row with half of your mesclun salad mix. Cover, firm, and water.

It is important that you keep these seed rows evenly moist until they germinate. Remember to plant the remaining half rows in two to three weeks to supply a steady stream of garden goodies.

Week Twelve (LATE APRIL) *Plant more lettuce and radishes.*

Continue planting the remaining half rows of radishes and lettuce just as you did before.

Week Thirteen (EARLY MAY) *Plant the remaining arugula and mesclun.*

Continue planting the remaining arugula and mesclun just as you did before. Pull any weeds that might be coming up and keep the garden watered if necessary.

Week Fourteen (EARLY MAY) *Thin lettuce; harvest radishes.*

It is important to thin the rows of lettuce and radishes so that they can grow to their full size. Simply remove as many lettuce plants as necessary from the row to leave 6 inches between each lettuce plant. Do the same with the radishes, leaving 1 inch between radish plants. These thinnings are wonderful accents to any salad.

Week Fifteen (MID-MAY) *Plant tomatoes, peppers, and eggplant.*

You shouldn't plant tomatoes, peppers, and eggplant in the garden until you are sure that there will be no chance of an overnight frost. These plants are very delicate, and a frost could damage or kill them. To protect your plants from a late frost, place a waxed-paper tomato cap, or dome, over each plant and weigh it down with rocks or soil. This not only prevents frost damage, it warms the soil during the day, which gives the plant a chance to grow rapidly during these still slightly cool days.

You are going to plant two each of tomato plants, yellow pepper plants, and eggplants. Please look at the planting diagram at the beginning of this chapter. Note that you are going to plant the cucumbers along the back row of the garden, so leave enough room for the trellis.

Place the plants on their spots 2 feet apart from one another in each direction. All of these are planted the same way. Using your hand trowel, dig a hole slightly larger and deeper than the root ball of the plant. Break up any clumps of soil and remove any rocks. Pour a tablespoon of natural organic fertilizer in each hole. Place the plant roots, peat pot and all, into the hole, firm the soil up and around the stem, and water. Continue with the rest of the plants.

Week Sixteen (LATE MAY) *Plant melons, beans, cucumbers, and herbs; harvest lettuce and mesclun.*

Plant Melons, Beans, and Cucumbers

Even though the melons I have suggested are only half the size of regular melons, they grow on vines that take up an area 2 feet in all directions around where you plant them. You are going to plant two circles, or "hills," of melons on the front right side of the garden. Smooth out two circles, each about 16 inches across, 2 feet from the front edge of the garden and 2 feet apart from one another. Arrange six melon seeds in a starlike, evenly-spaced pattern over the circles and poke the seeds down into the soil 1 inch deep. Cover with soil, firm down, and water.

Move back 2 feet from the melon circles and mark a 7-foot row. Dig a trench 1 inch deep along the row marker. Plant the bean seeds 2 inches apart in the row, cover with soil, firm, and water.

Build the 7-foot-long cucumber trellis along the back of the garden behind the tomato and pepper plants. Pound three stakes into the ground, one at either end and one in the middle of a 7-foot row. String the wire or mesh along the stakes and attach them with wire or string. Dig a trench $^1/_2$ inch deep along both sides of the fence. Plant the cucumber seeds 4 inches apart, cover with soil, firm down, and water.

Plant Herbs

Your gourmet culinary garden now lacks only a few herbs to be complete. Buy one or two French tarragon herb plants at your garden center and plant them in the front left corner of the garden. Tarragon is a perennial, which means it will return every year, spread, and get larger.

Plant as many of the six basil plants as you can find room for. Rather than confining them to a row, simply tuck them in next to the tomatoes, peppers, and eggplant rows.

For both tarragon and basil, use your hand trowel to dig holes slightly larger than the root ball of your herb plants. Place the root balls in the holes, firm the soil around them, and water.

Some other delicious and easy-growing herbs you might try to find room for are sorrel, chives, and parsley. Consider buying a small pot of each to accent your garden.

Harvest Lettuce and Mesclun

You should be able to harvest the most wonderful lettuce and beautiful mesclun greens right now. Simply remove a head of lettuce, roots and all, from the ground. Trim off the stem, wash and separate the leaves, and put the lettuce in a bowl. To harvest the mesclun, cut off bunches of the tops, leaving the stems in the ground where they will continue to grow more tops. Wash the leaves and add them to your salad. Add some of your fresh radishes, pour on your favorite dressing, toss, and serve.

Week Seventeen (EARLY JUNE) *Harvest peas.*

Petits pois are ready to harvest approximately sixty days from the day you planted them in the ground, which is just about now. You can tell if they are ready by feeling them for plumpness or opening a pod and looking inside. The peas should fill the pods. Pick as many peas as you want, shell the tiny peas, and toss the empty pods in the compost bin.

You can enjoy peas tossed with butter or steamed with a little bacon or ham and a touch of garlic. Try making this creamy soup, which is great hot or cold.

Fresh Pea Soup with Herbs

1 tablespoon unsalted butter or margarine

1 medium onion, peeled and chopped

3 cups shelled petits pois

2 cups canned or homemade chicken stock

2 tablespoons fresh minced herbs such as parsley, dill, thyme, salad burnet, chives, or a mixture

1 cup half-and-half

salt and pepper to taste

1. Melt the butter or margarine in a large saucepan over medium heat and saute the onions for three minutes. Add the peas and chicken stock, bring to a boil, reduce heat to medium low, and simmer for five minutes.

2. Place the mixture in a food processor and blend until smooth. Return to the saucepan and add the herbs, half-and-half, salt, and pepper. Simmer over low heat for five minutes; do not let boil. Add more salt and pepper if necessary.

3. Ladle the soup into bowls, sprinkle with a few more herbs, and serve.

Serves 4 to 6

Week Eighteen (MID-JUNE) *Install soaker hose; mulch the garden.*

Dry weather may have already hit your part of the country and you may have begun watering. The most water-conserving and effective way to water is with a soaker hose. Buy a 50-foot length of soaker hose and lace it through the garden in a modified S pattern. Fifty feet will be enough because this hose soaks the ground 18 inches on either side of its path.

Pull out any weeds that may have popped up and spread a 4- to 6-inch layer of straw or other mulch all over the garden. Get as close to the plants as you can, but don't crowd or smother them. You can lay the mulch right on top of the soaker hose.

Week Nineteen (MID- TO LATE JUNE) *Cage the tomatoes.*

In a small garden like yours, it is more space conserving to corral your tomatoes in upright cages rather than let them spread out and grow across the ground. It also helps prevent diseases. Simply buy two sturdy tomato cages at your garden center and lower them down over your tomato plants. Force the stakes into the ground to give the cage stability. As the tomatoes grow up, adjust their stems so that they are supported inside the cage by the cage wires.

Week Twenty (LATE JUNE TO EARLY JULY) *Fertilize the garden.*

At this point the plants in your garden have eaten up and utilized the fertilizer you gave them early in the season. Add a tablespoon or two of natural organic fertilizer at the base of every tomato, pepper, and eggplant, sprinkled in the circles of melons, and along the trellis of cucumbers. The rest of the plants don't need any extra fertilizer.

Week Twenty-one (EARLY TO MID-JULY) *Patrol for pests.*

Pests, especially insects, usually accompany the coming of really warm, dry weather. Your garden might not be attacked by any pests at all, but if it is, the best way to control pests is to watch for them by examining your plants on a daily or weekly basis, looking for damaging pests. If you find a problem, you may be able to control it by simply pulling the pests off by hand and squashing them. In addition there are some environmentally friendly sprays you can use to help you beat the bugs. For details please refer to the chapter Environmental Pest Control in Part 1.

Peas, lettuce, radish, carrots, beets, arugula, and mesclun are generally not attacked by bugs. Everything you have planted is resistant to diseases like wilt and virus, so it is hoped that you won't have any of these problems.

- Tomatoes: Look for hornworms, 1- to 2-inch-long pale green caterpillars. Spray with *Bt*.
- Cucumbers and melons: Look for cucumber beetles, half-inch long greenish-yellow bugs with black heads. Spray with pyrethrum or rotenone.
- Haricots verts: Look for Mexican bean beetles, $1/4$- to $1/2$-inch-long yellowish-brown bugs with black spots. Spray with rotenone or pyrethrum.

If you start having problems with bugs or diseases that are not covered in this book, consult your local county cooperative extension agent or garden center for more help and advice.

Week Twenty-two (MID- TO LATE JULY) *Water the garden; harvest beans and cucumbers.*

If your plants are beginning to wilt from lack of water, you should start watering. Simply attach a regular garden hose from your house spigot to the soaker hose, which you have already installed. Turn on the water and soak the garden for two to four hours. This slow watering should saturate the ground to a depth of 6 inches. If dry weather continues, water again on a weekly basis.

Haricots verts are slender little green beans that are about half the size of regular green beans. First your plants will flower and then start producing beans at a very rapid pace. It is important that you harvest haricots verts on an almost daily basis. The more you harvest them the more they produce. If you don't pick the beans when they are young, they grow long, get tough, and become inedible; in addition the plants begin to lose their vigor. Simply place the beans in a bag in the refrigerator until you have enough to cook with.

Niçoise Salad with Haricots Verts

There are as many different recipes for Salade Niçoise as there are cooks who make it, but when made in the summer, it should always feature haricots verts. This is how I remember its being served at the many charcuteries in and around Nice as I hitchhiked my way across the south of France one summer.

> *1 pound small, new red or white potatoes*
> *1 medium or 2 small tender zucchini, sliced into ¹/₂-inch chunks*
> *1 pound haricots verts*
> *1 pound fresh ripe tomatoes, cored and sliced*
> *2 anchovy strips or 1 teaspoon anchovy paste*
> *¹/₂ cup extra-virgin olive oil*
> *4 tablespoons white wine vinegar*
> *1 tablespoon tiny capers*
> *¹/₂ cup black Nicoise olives*
> *salt and pepper to taste*

1. Peel the potatoes and cut them in half. Put them in a large pot, cover them with an ample amount of water, and bring to a boil. Cover the pot and cook ten minutes.

2. Add the zucchini to the pot and cook one minute. Add the haricots verts and cook another minute. Drain the vegetables and cover them with cold water. Drain again and let cool.

3. To make the dressing, mash the anchovy filet in the bottom of a large mixing bowl. Add the vinegar and oil and stir to form a creamy dressing. Add the salt, pepper, capers, and olives and stir.

4. Add the vegetables to the dressing and stir to coat well. Add the tomatoes and stir gently to coat well. Let the salad stand covered at

room temperature for an hour for the flavors to mingle.

Serves 4 to 6 as a side dish, but if you add a can of tuna to the salad, it makes a full lunch for 2.

Fresh Cornichons
with Sour Cream Dressing

Many people think of cornichons as tiny pickles from a jar to be served with pâté and bread, but these miniature cucumbers are delicious served fresh in a salad.

> *12 fresh cornichons, 1 to 2 inches long*
> *1/2 cup sour cream or crème fraîche*
> *2 tablespoons finely chopped parsley or half parsley and half tarragon*
> *1 tablespoon scallions, finely chopped*
> *1 tablespoon fresh lemon juice*
> *4 large leaves garden lettuce, washed and dried*

1. Wash and trim the fresh cornichons. Slice them lengthwise in half. Slice each half into thin strips.

2. In a medium mixing bowl, stir the sour cream, parsley, scallion, and lemon juice together. Stir in the cornichons until coated. Refrigerate.

3. To serve, place a layer of lettuce on small, individual salad plates. Spoon the cucumber mixture into the center of each.

Serves 4

Week Twenty-three (LATE JULY TO EARLY AUGUST) *Harvest carrots.*

If you have prepared your garden soil the way I have suggested, your carrots should slip easily out of the ground when you tug on them. If they resist, it means that your soil is still too hard and that next year you will need to add additional organic matter to loosen the soil up. Another trick is to add a 1-pound coffee can full of ordinary sand, not salty seaside sand, to the area where you plan to plant your carrots. Sand really helps loosen the soil. Once you have mastered the soil, you will find the sweet taste of your own home-grown carrots worth the little bit of extra effort.

Braised Baby Carrots

These carrots are so tender that they don't really need peeling. Just give them a good scrubbing to remove the dirt.

> *1 pound baby carrots, washed and pared*
> *1 tablespoon unsalted butter or margarine*
> *1 teaspoon minced fresh tarragon leaves*
> *1 cup chicken stock*
> *1 teaspoon country-style French mustard*
> *salt and pepper to taste*

1. Place the carrots in a 1-quart saucepan. Add the butter or margarine, the fresh tarragon, and the chicken stock.

2. Cover the pan and simmer over medium heat for ten minutes or until the carrots are tender. Don't overcook.

3. Add the mustard, salt, and pepper and stir. Heat for one minute and serve.

Serves 4 as a side dish

Week Twenty-four (MID-AUGUST) *Harvest tomatoes.*

It is really a culinary wonder of nature that tomatoes and fresh basil come into season at the same time in the garden. Their flavors are just made for each other.

Everybody has their favorite way of serving and eating tomatoes. The following recipe is mine.

Mediterranean Tomatoes with Fresh Basil

The tomatoes and basil are so fresh that I suggest you try to buy freshly made mozzarella, which is soft and tender like a little pillow of cheese rather than rubbery and firm like ordinary pizza mozzarella. Ask for it at an Italian food market or gourmet store, although you might find some at the specialty cheese section of your supermarket.

> *4 large, ripe tomatoes*
> *1 pound fresh mozzarella*
> *16 leaves of fresh Genovese basil*
> *¼ cup extra-virgin olive oil*
> *2 tablespoons balsamic or red wine vinegar*
> *salt and pepper to taste*

1. Core the tomatoes and slice them into ¼-inch slices.

2. Slice the mozzarella into ¼-inch slices.

3. Arrange the tomatoes and mozzarella on a large serving plate in an alternating pattern of one tomato slice overlapping one mozzarella slice and so on.

4. Arrange the basil leaves around the edges of the tomatoes and cheese, tucking them in under the slices. I find whole basil leaves to be a lot prettier than chopped or minced ones.

5. Drizzle the vinegar and the olive oil over the salad and dust with salt and pepper to taste.

6. Place the salad plate on the table and let people help themselves. This dish, along with a few slices of salami, a loaf of Italian bread, and a bowl of minestrone, makes a wonderful meal alfresco.

Serves 4

Week Twenty-five (LATE AUGUST) *Harvest and grill peppers and eggplant.*

Grilling peppers and eggplants, especially over a charcoal grill, really brings out a smoky, gutsy flavor of these vegetables that is hidden when you use other cooking methods. Some cookbooks tell you to remove the charred skin from grilled peppers, but I never do.

Grilled Peppers and Eggplants

4 to 6 yellow bell peppers
4 to 6 white or purple eggplants
4 tablespoons extra-virgin olive oil
2 tablespoons balsamic or red wine vinegar
salt and pepper to taste

1. Preheat your broiler or prepare a barbecue grill until the coals are white.

2. Cut the peppers in half and remove the seeds. Cut the eggplants in half. Place the eggplants and the peppers under the boiler or on the grill for about ten minutes. Turn often and brush lightly with 1 tablespoon olive oil.

3. Place the vegetables on a plate, drizzle with remaining olive oil, vinegar, salt, and pepper and serve.

Serves 4 as an appetizer

Week Twenty-six (EARLY SEPTEMBER) *Harvest melons.*

The first time I ate a small, aromatic, Charentais-type melon I was riding my motorcycle back to Spain from France in late August. They were so good that I spent an extra day in town just so I could eat more of them.

Very few people do anything with melons but slice them open and eat them fresh and completely unadorned. If you feel like doing something fancy and showcasing your melons in a unique summer salad, however, here's a recipe that makes a full luncheon meal.

Chicken, Melon, and Avocado Salad with Lime-Hazelnut Dressing

2 whole boneless, skinless chicken breasts

1 head Buttercrunch or Bibb lettuce from the garden

2 ripe avocados

2 ripe melons from your garden

1 large red bell pepper

³/₄ cup hazelnuts

1 cup light olive oil

5 tablespoons fresh lime juice

2 tablespoons fresh parsley or tarragon, minced

salt and pepper to taste

1. Broil the chicken breasts for three minutes on each side or until just done. Don't overcook. Cool and slice the breasts across the grain into ¹/₄-inch-thick pieces.

2. Wash and dry the lettuce and tear into bite-sized pieces.

3. Peel and slice the avocado and melon into ¹/₄-inch-thick slices. Core the pepper and slice into very thin strips.

4. Toast the hazelnuts in a skillet for ten minutes over low heat until they begin to brown and become fragrant. Rub the skins off and place in a food processor. (If you can buy ground hazelnuts, skip these steps.) Add the oil, lime juice, salt, pepper, and herbs. Blend to form a creamy dressing.

5. Assemble the salad on individual plates by spreading some lettuce on each plate and arranging the chicken, melon, avocado, and pepper slices over it. Drizzle with dressing and serve.

Serves 4

Week Twenty-seven (SEPTEMBER TO FIRST HARD FROST) *Prepare the garden for winter.*

Don't get me wrong. Your garden season is far from being over. Your garden will continue to provide you with tomatoes, peppers, eggplant, and other delights all the way up until frost, but it is time to start thinking about cooler weather and preparing your garden for winter.

As your plants finish their seasons, pull them up and toss them in the compost bin. It is better if you can shred the larger plants a little bit, but don't worry if you can't. Spread whatever organic matter or mulch you might have left over on the garden. When the leaves fall, rake a 4- to 6-inch layer of leaves over the garden. All of this organic matter will begin to decay over the winter and add richness to your soil. In the spring you can till it in and have another great garden season.

An Old-Fashioned Heirloom Garden

*T*his Old-Fashioned Heirloom Garden is going to be the most culturally interesting garden you will grow from this book. You will learn something about the horticultural history of American gardening because you are going to plant some of the same seeds that the Native Americans, seventeenth- and eighteenth-century colonists, and nineteenth-century immigrants did.

In one patch of your garden, you will plant a Colonial garden of corn, beans, and pumpkin—three vegetables that are native to the New World—in a style the Native Americans taught the English colonists. You will also grow parsnips, the "potato" of Europe before the potato was discovered; watermelons, popular with the Amish; a unique tomato; German lettuce, an icicle radish; a variety of cantaloupe named after a nineteenth-century actress; English peas; Hamburg parsley; white squash; and Egyptian beets. And you will be able to use your own pumpkin for pumpkin pie on Thanksgiving.

The seeds of all these vegetables and fruits were grown before the great hybrid revolution in the 1940s, when agricultural geneticists began breeding

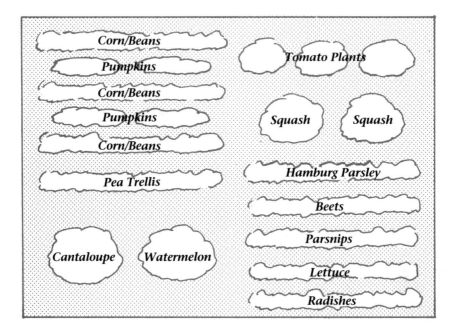

seeds to make them more vigorous and productive. These are the seeds that modern agriculture has forgotten. By planting them in your garden, you will be preserving genetic diversity and growing a piece of history.

Many heirloom varieties do not have the disease resistance of modern varieties. I have, however, carefully selected the varieties that are the least likely to be affected by disease. In addition, the rich organic soil you are going to prepare for your garden does a very good job of preventing diseases all by itself.

Although this garden is fairly pest resistant, I will give you specific instructions on controlling pests in the most environmentally sound way possible. You'll have the fun of starting your own tomato seedlings indoors on a windowsill in early March. The biggest problem will be keeping the vines of your pumpkin and melon plants from roaming out of the garden and onto the lawn.

Besides the wonderful seeds you are going to buy, you will need the following supplies for your garden: six $2^1/_4$-inch peat pots, a small bag of potting soil, a mini-greenhouse, four 40-pound bags of compost, a 4-cubic-foot bag of peat moss, a 2- to 5-pound bag of blended natural organic fertilizer, three 5-foot-long wooden or metal stakes, and a 7-foot-long, 3- to 4-foot-high length of fencing wire for your pea fence, three hot caps, and three tomato cages. You will also need the tools outlined in the earlier chapter on garden tools and three to four bales of straw for mulch.

The Weekly Guide

Week One (LATE JANUARY) *Order your seed catalogs.*

The only way you can buy some of these seeds is through catalogs that specialize in heirloom seeds. Some of the seeds are easy to find; in fact, I bought a packet of Scarlet Runner beans off the rack at my local garden center last year. I suggest you order several of the catalogs listed here because they are usually full of in-depth historical and cultural information about the seeds and because they have nifty old-fashioned pictures in them. Another reason to order from these catalog companies is that they are doing the necessary work of preserving these forgotten seeds and they need your help. Send a postcard or letter to the following:

- Heirloom Seeds, P.O. Box 245, West Elizabeth, PA 15088–0245; no telephone; $1.00 charge for catalog. Excellent selection of seeds at good prices.
- J. W. Jung Seed Co., 335 High Street, Randolph, WI 53957. Great selection of heirloom and modern seeds.
- Plants of the Southwest, 930 Baca Street, Santa Fe, NM 87501; $1.50 charge for catalog. Neat selection of hot chili peppers and beans collected from Native Americans.
- R. H. Shumway's, P.O. Box 1, Graniteville, SC 29829. Old family seed business established in Rockford, Illinois in 1870. Old Sears catalog-type pictures and home of the Abraham Lincoln tomato.
- Seeds Blum, Idaho City Stage, Boise, ID 83706; $2.00 charge for catalog.
- Southern Exposure Seed Exchange, P.O. Box 158, North Garden, VA 22959; $3.00 charge for catalog. One of the most extensive heirloom catalogs, full of valuable information; many varieties are selected for mid-Atlantic and mid-South gardeners, but most are applicable to all the United States.

Week Two (EARLY FEBRUARY) *Survey your friends and family.*

Even though I am going to give you specific suggestions for which seeds to buy, I think it would be a good idea to ask your friends and family if they have any favorites they want you to grow. Besides getting everyone interested in what you are doing, you might get some help from them pulling weeds later on.

Week Three (MID-FEBRUARY) *Place your seed order.*

Once you get your seed catalogs and start reading the colorful names and descriptions of the various seeds, my list is probably going to go out the window. I will give you a few choices, but feel free to choose your favorite seeds within the categories I've listed below. Buy one packet each of the following varieties:

- Beans: Scarlet Runner, Old Homestead, Lazy Wife, Kentucky Wonder, or Genuine Cornfield. These are known as pole beans because gardeners usually train them to grow on 8-foot high poles. Noted for their beany flavor, these are the beans you will grow in the Colonial portion of your garden. Scarlet Runner beans have beautiful flowers that attract hummingbirds.

- Beets: Early Blood, Detroit Dark Red, Crosby's Dark Red Egyptian. All these are popular nineteenth-century varieties, when beets were called "blood turnips."

- Cantaloupe: Jenny Lind, Rocky Ford or Green Nutmeg if you like green flesh; Delicious 51, Hearts of Gold, or Old Time Tennessee if you like salmon-colored flesh. Delicious flavor of how cantaloupes used to taste when I was a boy growing up along the banks of the Sangamon and melons were four for $1.00.

- Corn: Country Gentleman, also called Shoepeg, an 1891 white variety with irregular rows of kernels; Stowell's Evergreen, white corn developed before the Civil War with its roots in original Indian corn; or Golden Bantam, a yellow corn introduced at the turn of the century.

- Lettuce: Schweitzer's Mesher Bibb, White Boston, Tom Thumb, Black-Seeded Simpson, Prizehead, or Grand Rapids. Bibb, Boston, and Tom Thumb all form small heads of lettuce, whereas the other three are easy-to-grow leaf lettuces.

- Hamburg parsley; also called rooted parsley: This is a dual-purpose vegetable. The underground, white-fleshed root has the same parsley-like flavor as the curled green parsley tops that grow above ground. Just pretend you are growing white carrots that taste like parsley.

- Parsnips: Hollow Crown, Harris Model, or Fullback. Long before Europeans ate potatoes, they ate parsnips. A wonderful vegetable that tastes quite sweet when it is roasted along with a leg of lamb or a loin of beef.

- English peas: Alderman, Lincoln, Thomas Laxton, Homesteader, Dark Green Perfection, Little Marvel, or Blue Bantam. These pea vines grow 3 to 4 feet tall and need a fence to grow on. Each pod contains seven to nine full-flavored dark-green peas that kids love to help shell.

- Pumpkins: New England, Small Sugar, or Pie Pumpkin. These sweeter, orange-fleshed pumpkins weigh only 5 to 8 pounds, unlike the 25-pound monsters used for making jack-o'-lanterns. Even though they are tiny, they can still be decorated but are difficult to carve. Try the Connecticut Field Pumpkin if you want both a good pie and a good jack-o'-lantern pumpkin.
- Radish: White Icicle, Lady Finger, Sparkler, Crimson or German Giant, or French Breakfast. Radishes are always the earliest vegetable ready in the garden and early settlers looked forward to their crispy crunch after a long winter.
- Summer squash: Early White Bush Scallop or White Patty Pan. These are round, slightly flat, deeply scalloped squash that were introduced before 1722. They grow and are eaten like zucchini.
- Tomato: Mortgage Lifter, Money Maker, German Johnson, Pritchard Scarlet Topper, Oxheart, Jefferson Giant, Red Brandywine, or, for you midwestern growers, Abraham Lincoln, available only in the Shumway catalog.
- Watermelon: Amish Moon & Stars or Moon & Stars are 25- to 40-pound red-fleshed melons with dark-green rind mottled with yellow spots that resemble moons and stars. Other great choices are Tom Watson, Klecky Sweets, Crimson Sweet, or Rattlesnake.

Week Four (MID- TO LATE FEBRUARY) *Choose your garden site.*

Your garden will measure 10 feet deep by 15 feet long. Look for a site that is on level ground and gets full sunshine for at least six hours every day. Eight to ten hours of sunshine is even better. Now is a good time to trim excess tree branches or shrubs to get rid of shade.

Your garden needs to be well drained. Look for a site that never has puddles or standing water on it at any time of the year. Choose a site that is fairly close to the house so that you can reach it with a hose and don't have to walk so far to carry things back and forth.

Week Five (LATE FEBRUARY) *Choose a place indoors to start plants; buy your seed-starting supplies.*

In a week or so, you are going to start your own heirloom tomato plants indoors in preparation for planting them outdoors in June. When the seeds are first planted indoors, they need a warm place to germinate. Look for a place in your home that keeps a temperature of at least 70 degrees F. I usually place my seedlings on a sunny windowsill in my kitchen.

Since you are only planting tomato seeds, all you need are six $2^1/_4$-inch peat pots, a small bag of potting soil, and a mini-greenhouse in which to grow them. Most garden centers sell mini-greenhouses made of plastic, and I really find my mini-greenhouse to be a very effective and inexpensive place to germinate seeds.

Week Six (EARLY MARCH) *Start your tomato plants indoors.*

In late May or early June, when you plant your tomato plants outside, you will have room in your garden for only three plants, but I want you to start six seedlings in case of growth failure or an accident, such as knocking one over. In all likelihood you will have three extra heirloom tomato plants that any neighbor or friend would gladly accept as a gift.

Fill the peat pots almost full of potting soil and press down lightly. Place four tomato seeds, evenly spaced, with one in the middle, on top of the soil. Cover with 1 teaspoon of potting soil and press down lightly. Spoon 1 tablespoon of water on top of the soil and place the planted peat pot in the mini-greenhouse. Repeat with the remaining peat pots. Place the cover on the greenhouse and keep the pots warm and watered until the seedlings sprout.

Week Seven (EARLY MARCH) *Keep your plants warm and watered.*

Check your mini-greenhouse every day to be sure the pots are warm and watered. They need to be moist but not soggy. A warm room with a little bit of sunshine every day should be adequate.

When they sprout, be sure to ventilate the mini-greenhouse by opening the vent in the roof or by adjusting the top so it is slightly ajar. This will prevent heat from building up inside and killing the seedlings.

Week Eight (MID-MARCH) *Thin your seedlings.*

The time to thin your tomato seedlings is when they are about 2 inches tall and have their second set of leaves. Leave one stout sprout in each pot. Locate the strongest sprout and remove the rest by pulling gently or cutting them off at soil level with a sharp knife or scissors.

Week Nine (MID- TO LATE MARCH) *Prepare the garden soil.*

As soon as the snow has cleared and the soil has thawed or dried out from winter rains, prepare your garden soil. First mark off an area 10 feet wide and 15 feet long and remove any grass or sod that is growing there. Clear the area of any rocks, sticks, and debris.

Go to your garden center and buy four 40-pound bags of compost or composted manure, one 4-cubic-foot bag of sphagnum peat moss, and a 2- to 5-pound box or bag of balanced natural organic fertilizer. If you can buy only a 10-pound bag of fertilizer, go ahead. You will use a lot of it this year, and it will store quite well for use next year.

Dig the area to a depth of at least 8 inches. You can do this by hand with a forked spade or you can till the ground with a rotary tiller. You can rent a tiller for the day or hire a person to come by and do it for you. Look in the Yellow Pages or classifieds. Be sure to break up any clumps and remove any rocks.

Open the bags of compost and sphagnum peat moss and spread them evenly over the garden. Following the manufacturer's instructions, spread the correct amount of fertilizer on your garden. In general a 1-pound coffee can of fertilizer will be the correct amount. Till the entire area again, working the organic matter and fertilizer into the soil to a depth of at least 4 inches.

Rake the soil smooth, and you are ready to plant.

Week Ten (EARLY APRIL) *Begin planting peas, radishes, and lettuce.*

Please refer to the garden design at the beginning of this chapter. You are going to build a pea fence and plant peas in the middle of the left half of your garden, which is directly in front of the Colonial garden and behind the melon patch. Don't worry. By the time the corn and melons start growing, your peas will have been harvested; then you can either remove the pea fence or just leave it there.

First build a pea fence. Using your string-and-stakes row marker, mark a 7-foot-long row horizontally in the middle of the left side of your garden. Drive three stakes in the ground along the row, one at either end and one in the middle. Stretch the fence along the stakes and secure the fence to the stakes with wire or string. Dig a trench 1-inch deep along the base of the fence on either side. Plant the peas in the trenches, spacing the seeds 2 inches apart. Cover the seeds with soil, firm down with your hand, and water with a watering can.

To plant the radishes, mark a 7-foot-long row on the front right side of the garden, 1 foot in from the edge. Dig a trench $1/2$ inch deep and plant half the radish seeds, spaced 1 inch apart. You will plant the remaining radish seeds in two weeks so that all of your radishes aren't ready to eat at the same time. Cover the seeds with soil, firm down, and water.

To plant the lettuce, move back from the radishes 1 foot and mark a row 7 feet long. Dig a trench $1/4$ to $1/2$ inch deep and sprinkle lettuce seeds in half the row. Cover with soil, firm down, and water. You will plant the rest of the lettuce seeds in two to three weeks to ensure a steady supply of lettuce.

Be sure to water the seeds almost every day to keep them moist but not soggy until they germinate in about a week to ten days.

Week Eleven (MID-APRIL) *Plant parsnips, beets, and parsley.*

To plant the parsnips, move back from the lettuce row 1 foot. Mark a row 7 feet long and dig a trench $1/2$ inch deep. Sprinkle the parsnip seeds in the row, leaving 1 inch between seeds. Cover with soil, firm down, and water.

To plant the beets, move back from the parsnip row 1 foot and mark a 7-foot row. Dig a trench $1/2$ inch deep and plant the beet seeds, leaving 1 inch between seeds. Cover with soil, firm down, and water.

To plant the Hamburg parsley, move back from the beet row 1 foot and mark a 7-foot-long row. Dig a trench $1/2$ inch deep, plant the parsley seeds 1 inch apart in the row, cover with soil, firm down, and water.

Remember to keep these newly planted rows watered every day until germination. Water the radishes, peas, and lettuce, too. Be sure to use the watering can because water from a hose may be strong enough to dislodge the seeds from their rows.

Week Twelve (LATE APRIL) *Thin plants; replant.*

You don't need to thin the peas you have planted, but thinning does make a difference in the quality of lettuce and radishes you will harvest. Pull out enough tiny lettuce plants to leave a 4-inch space between the remaining plants. Pull enough tiny radish plants to leave a 2-inch space between the remaining radishes. These thinnings may be tiny, but they make a great addition to your salad bowl.

Now is the time to plant the second half of your radish and lettuce rows. Dig a $1/2$-inch trench as you did before, sprinkle the seeds in the row, cover with soil, firm down, and water with a watering can.

Week Thirteen (EARLY MAY) *Begin harvesting radishes.*

For the freshest, sweetest, and juiciest radishes, start harvesting them now. As the weather warms up, they may get pithy and more piquant. You don't need to harvest all of them at once. Simply pull up the ones you want to eat, wash them, and serve them. The French like to make radish sandwiches by slicing them thinly and layering them on a baguette spread with unsalted butter. It tastes really good.

Remember to keep all your rows watered and to pull any weeds that may be popping up here and there.

Week Fourteen (MID-MAY) *Begin harvesting lettuce.*

The lettuce that you planted is now ready for you to begin harvesting. Pick the largest heads, giving the remaining heads more room to grow. Wash them and toss with your favorite salad fixings.

Week Fifteen (LATE MAY) *Plant the Colonial garden.*

Kids love this part of the garden. My son helped me plant our Colonial corn, bean, and pumpkin patch this year—we love watching these magnificent and colorful plants grow and prosper. The seeds for this patch are all very large, and the rows don't have to be straight, so the kids can easily plant this section and make it theirs.

Please look at the garden diagram at the beginning of this chapter. You are going to plant the corn, runner beans, and pumpkins all together in a section 5 feet wide and 7 feet long at the back left side of the garden.

Using your string-and-stakes row marker, mark three rows for the corn, 7-feet long, 1 foot apart, starting 1 foot in from the back left side of the garden. Dig 1-inch-deep trenches along each row marker and plant the corn, leaving 4 inches between seed kernels. To help you see where you are going in this section, don't cover the kernels with soil until after you have planted the beans and pumpkin seeds.

Plant the bean seeds 1 foot apart in the same rows as you planted the corn seeds. Simply poke the bean seeds (big, aren't they?) down into the soil 1 inch deep.

Plant the pumpkin seeds 18 inches apart in the spaces between the corn rows. Poke them down into the soil 1-inch deep.

Now cover all the seeds with soil, firm down the entire area by pounding the flat side of a garden rake over the space, and water well with a watering can. Keep the patch watered until the seeds germinate in a week to ten days.

Week Sixteen (LATE MAY TO EARLY JUNE) *Plant watermelon and cantaloupe.*

Plant the watermelon and cantaloupe in the other half of the left side of the garden across the pea fence from the corn and beans (see diagram at beginning of chapter). You are going to plant the melons in two circles, known as hills. Melon vines spread several feet in all directions, so you will need plenty of room.

Use the rake handle and divide the remaining quadrant in half. In the middle of the two halves, draw two circles, 12 inches across. Plant five cantaloupe seeds in a starlike pattern in one "hill," and repeat the process with watermelon seeds in the other hill. Poke all the seeds down into the soil, cover with soil, firm down with your hand, and water.

Remember to keep the seeds watered until they germinate.

Week Seventeen (EARLY JUNE) *Plant tomatoes and squash.*

It doesn't do any good to transplant tomatoes or plant squash seeds until all danger of frost has passed in your area and until the soil is very warm. Now is a good time. Please refer to the garden diagram at the beginning of this chapter.

Place three tomato plants equally spaced along the back right side of your garden, 1 foot in from the back edge and 1 foot in from either side. Using a hand trowel, dig a hole slightly larger and deeper than the peat pots. Sprinkle a tablespoon of balanced natural organic fertilizer in the hole and stir it around a little. Place the peat pot in the hole, gather the soil up around the stem, firm the soil gently, and water. Place a waxed-paper cone called a "hot cap" over each of the three tomato plants and weigh the caps down with rocks to hold them in place against the wind. These caps not only protect your plants from frost, they act as little greenhouses that trap heat and give the tomato plants a needed boost. Leave the caps on for a week or so, peeking underneath once in a while to make sure your tomatoes are doing well, and then remove them.

Plant the squash in two circles, also called hills, evenly spaced in the next row 18 inches away from the tomato plants. Draw two circles 12 inches across and plant five seeds in a starlike pattern. Poke the seeds into the ground 1 inch, cover with soil, firm down, and water.

Week Eighteen (MID-JUNE) *Harvest beets.*

In the nineteenth century gardeners let roots grow as large as softballs and then stored them in the root cellar for eating in winter. For today's gardener the best time to harvest beets is when they are still young and tender, sized larger than a golf ball but still smaller than a baseball. Pull them up from the ground, trim off the tops, and wash them. Don't peel them until after they are cooked.

The simplest way to enjoy beets is to simmer them in a pan of water for fifteen to twenty minutes, slip their peels off, slice them up, and dot with butter. When they are cold, you can grate them and add them to a salad. Many people, myself included, marvel at the wonderfully sweet taste of beets that have been baked in the oven for an hour. Try it sometime.

Week Nineteen (MID-JUNE) *Harvest peas.*

If you wish, you can leave the peas on their vines until they dry out and then store them for use in pea soup the way our ancestors did, but I prefer to eat my peas fresh.

For the following recipe, you'll need to pick enough pods to fill a 4-quart pot. Then start shelling by pulling the strings off and cracking the pods open. Put the pods in the compost pile.

Creamed Peas with Ham

Creamed peas was a very popular dish in Colonial times, even gracing the tables of George Washington and Thomas Jefferson. The addition of cured ham is also traditional and gives the peas wonderful flavor.

> *3 cups fresh peas, shelled*
> *1 cup smoked ham, finely cubed*
> *1 tablespoon unsalted butter or margarine*
> *1 tablespoon flour*
> *1 cup milk*
> *salt and pepper to taste*
> *1 tablespoon finely minced parsley, chives, or other fresh herb*

1. Place the peas in a 2- to 3-quart saucepan. Cover with water and bring to a boil. Reduce the heat to medium and simmer for five to eight minutes. Drain.

2. Add the cubed ham to the peas and stir. Add the butter or margarine and let it melt. Stir. Add the flour and stir to coat well. Add the milk and simmer to form a creamy gravy. Add salt and pepper to taste.

3. Pour the peas into a serving bowl and sprinkle with fresh herbs.

Serves 4 as a side dish

Week Twenty (LATE JUNE) *Cage the tomatoes; install soaker hose; weed and mulch the garden.*

Remove the tomato caps from the tomato plants if you haven't already. Lower the tomato cages over the tomato plants and arrange the leaves to drape over the first rung.

The best way to water your garden and conserve water at the same time is by using a soaker hose. Soaker hoses drip water out so slowly that none is lost to runoff. Simply lace the soaker hose around your garden in an S pattern and leave it there all summer. When you want to water, just hook a regular connecting hose between the soaker and the spigot on the house.

Mulch your garden using the straw you bought at the garden center. If you have access to another type of mulch such as shredded leaves or pine needles, please feel free to use what you want. Straw is good because it is attractive and it doesn't contain millions of seeds that might sprout next year as noxious weeds. Spread a 4- to 6-inch layer of straw between the rows, around the plants, and under the vines. Pull any weeds that may have popped up. The more straw you put down, the fewer weeds you will have to pull later on. Place the straw right over the soaker hose. This mulch will conserve water, stifle weeds, keep the garden soil cool, and decompose like compost to improve your garden soil. It is very important.

Week Twenty-one (EARLY JULY) *Watch for pests.*

Be sure to keep eating radishes, peas, beets, and lettuce. Together they make a tasty vegetable salad with your favorite vinaigrette.

By adding organic matter to your soil, watering conservatively, feeding with natural organic fertilizers, and not using chemical sprays, you have done a lot to make your garden a disease- and pest-resistant place. Nevertheless, a few bugs may find their way into your garden despite your best efforts. At this time of year, you should be examining your plants for bugs whenever you go to the garden. This is called "scouting" in agriculture. Here's what pests to look for and how to control them in the most environmentally friendly way:

Squash vine borer: 1-inch-long white caterpillar with a brown head that bores into the vines near the base. Dust with Bacillus thuringiensis.

Tomato hornworm: 3- to 4-inch-long green caterpillar. Pick off by hand or spray with pyrethrum.

Corn borer: 1-inch-long grayish-pink caterpillar. Spray or dust with rotenone or pyrethrum.

Mexican bean beetle: $1/2$-inch-long bug with yellow/brown shell with black spots. Don't confuse it with a ladybug, which has a distinctive orange shell. Spray or dust with rotenone or pyrethrum.

Japanese beetle: $1/2$-inch-long bluish-green beetle. Spray or dust with rotenone or pyrethrum.

Please read the chapter in this book on environmental pest control. Always read and follow carefully the package labels of all biological and botanical pest controls.

Week Twenty-two (MID-JULY) *Fertilize and water the garden; harvest Hamburg parsley.*

By now your garden has used up most of the fertilizer you added early in the season. Now is the time to add some more. Place 1 tablespoon of balanced natural organic fertilizer at the base of each tomato plant, 2 tablespoons distributed among each hill of melons and squash, and 1 cup sprinkled evenly around the Colonial patch. The rest of your vegetables don't need any more fertilizer.

Unless you have been getting ample rainfall, about 1 inch per week, you probably need to start watering your garden. Simply hook the soaker hose up to the regular hose that you have run out from the spigot on the house. Turn on the water halfway and let it run for two to four hours. This will provide enough water to saturate the soil in your garden to a depth of 6 to 8 inches.

Don't water again for another week. Slow but infrequent waterings make your garden more drought-resistant than quick but frequent waterings.

Hamburg Parsley
with Potatoes au Gratin

You can start snipping off sprigs of parsley from your Hamburg parsley any time now. In fact, some of the roots are ready to eat now, too.

> *2 to 3 medium Hamburg parsley roots*
> *2 to 3 medium all-purpose white potatoes*
> *1 tablespoon butter*
> *¹/₂ cup milk or half-and-half*
> *salt and pepper to taste*
> *3 tablespoons Parmesan cheese*
> *1 tablespoon minced parsley*

1. Wash and peel the potatoes and parsley roots. Chop them coarsely and place them in a pan of water. Bring to a boil and simmer for fifteen minutes or until roots are soft.

2. Drain the roots and add the butter, milk, salt, and pepper. Mash the roots just as if you were making mashed potatoes.

3. Spread the mixture into a small, ovenproof baking dish, sprinkle with cheese and parsley, and place under the broiler until the cheese melts and a light-brown crust forms on top.

Serves 4 as a side dish

Week Twenty-three (LATE JULY) *Harvest runner beans.*

If you really wanted to produce a bumper crop of beans, you would have staked these vines up on a 10-foot fence. But I think this garden has much more aesthetic appeal than a fence. Pick the beans by pulling them from the vines when they are 4 to 6 inches long and before the beans inside the pods swell and get large.

Potato, Runner Beans, and Vidalia Onion Salad

1 pound red or white new potatoes

1 pound Scarlet Runner beans

1 large Vidalia, Walla Walla, Texas Sweet, or Maui onion

2 teaspoons Dijon mustard

salt and pepper to taste

2 tablespoons red wine, balsamic, or other flavored vinegar

6 tablespoons olive oil

1 teaspoon minced fresh rosemary or thyme

1. Simmer the potatoes in a pan of water until they are just tender. Don't overcook. Drain and peel if desired.

2. Trim off the stems of the beans and place them in a pan of water. Simmer until just tender. Drain and cool.

3. Peel the onion and slice into thin rings.

4. In the bottom of a large mixing bowl, add the Dijon mustard, salt, pepper, and wine vinegar. Stir to form a creamy paste. Add the olive oil in a steady stream and whisk to form a creamy dressing.

5. Add the potatoes, beans, and onion rings to the dressing and toss to coat well. Transfer to a serving bowl and sprinkle with the fresh herbs.

Serves 4

Week Twenty-four (LATE JULY) *Harvest squash.*

If you allow the squash to grow to their full 7-inch-diameter size, they tend to get tough and full of seeds. Instead, pick them when they are young by severing them at the base of the stem with a sharp knife.

Scalloped Squash
Stewed with Tomatoes

2 to 3 medium patty pan or white bush scallop squash
1 medium onion, peeled and chopped
2 to 3 medium fresh ripe tomatoes, peeled and chopped
1 tablespoon unsalted butter or margarine
salt and pepper to taste
1 tablespoon fresh minced parsley, thyme, chives, or other herb
  as garnish

1. Cut the squash in half and then cut each half into $1/2$-inch-thick wedges. Cut the onion in the same way. Peel the tomato by coring it first and then placing it in a pan of boiling water for ten seconds. Remove from the water, and the skin will peel right off. Drain out most of the juice and seeds and cut in the same way as the squash and onions.

2. Melt the butter or margarine in a large skillet. Add the onion and saute for two minutes. Add the squash and sauté for one minute. Add the tomatoes and simmer the vegetables for five minutes on medium heat.

3. Add the salt and pepper to taste and pour the vegetables into a serving bowl. Sprinkle with fresh herbs.

Serves 4 as a side dish

Week Twenty-five (EARLY AUGUST) *Harvest corn.*

Corn is ready to pick just when the silks are beginning to lose their color and turn brown. You can also carefully slip open an ear and look at the kernels. If they are large, well formed, full of juice, and bright with color, they are ready. Corn deteriorates very rapidly, so cook it as soon as you can.

Unfortunately, sweet corn is one of the favorite foods of deer, raccoons, and birds. If you fear you may have a problem with any of these critters, you need to defend you corn crop. The only reliable way to deter raccoons and deer is with a sturdy electric fence. To protect corn from birds drape a lightweight fabric netting over the corn just as the ears are beginning to form. You can find netting and electric fencing at most garden centers.

Roasted Corn in the Husk

Corn roasted in its husk over an open fire outdoors was the way fresh corn was eaten for hundreds of years. It still is one of the best.

> *2 ears of corn for each person*
> *butter or margarine*
> *salt and pepper to taste*
> *chili powder or paprika (optional)*

1. Prepare your gas or charcoal barbecue grill.

2. Pick two ears of corn for each person. Carefully peel back the husks, but don't tear them off. Remove all the silks.

3. Spread the uncooked ears of corn with melted butter or margarine and season with salt and pepper (chili powder or paprika is good also). Put the corn husks back over the ears of corn and tie with a little piece of string.

4. Lay the ears of corn, husks and all, on the grill. Baste with water, close the lid, and roast for fifteen minutes. Turn the ears and baste with water every five minutes. Depending on the heat of your fire, the husks will get grill marks, start to get dry, and even turn brown. Check to see if the corn is hot enough to eat and serve. Now you can tear the husks off and throw them away.

Week Twenty-six (MID-AUGUST) *Harvest tomatoes; keep watering; train pumpkin and melon vines.*

Keep watering once a week. Pull any weeds that might pop through and add a little extra mulch in any problem spots. Your garden may look a little overgrown right now with the melon and pumpkin vines running all over the place. Try to train them to stay in the garden by pointing the tips back into the garden.

Your tomatoes should be turning red and ripe by now, and you can start picking as soon as they are. Don't wait for them to get overripe and fall off the vine. In my opinion refrigerating tomatoes ruins their flavor. It's better to pick tomatoes when they are ripe and give them away to neighbors rather than trying to store them in the refrigerator.

Week Twenty-seven (LATE AUGUST) *Harvest melons.*

Many people find it difficult to know when a melon, especially a watermelon, is ripe and ready to pick. Here's how: A watermelon is ripe when the underside turns from white to yellow, orange, or gold. Usually the stem is shriveling at this point, too. If you have a good ear, the thumping method might work for you. It goes like this: Thump your own head; if the melon makes the same sound when thumped, it is underripe. Thump your chest; if the melon sounds like this, it is ripe. Thump your thigh; if the melon sounds like this, it is overripe. I wouldn't rely on the thumping method too much if I were you.

A cantaloupe is ripe when you can smell the aroma of the delicious fruit inside, when it begins to feel slightly soft to the touch, and when the stem drops off with the slightest pull.

I think everyone knows how to eat melons. A melon tastes best when it is harvested in the morning and placed in the shade all day or harvested late in the evening and left outside overnight. I like to serve cantaloupe Spanish style, in very thin slices (with the rind still on) that you carve and eat with a knife and fork. I like to serve watermelon Lebanese style, cut out of the rind, seeds removed, and cut into thin slices that are layered on a plate. Serving melons in this way adds a little elegance to the fruit.

Week Twenty-eight (EARLY SEPTEMBER) *Keep harvesting parsnips.*

You could have harvested some of your parsnips two weeks ago, but they keep well in the ground and actually improve in flavor as cool weather approaches. Parsnips can be steamed and mashed with potatoes or baked with a roast or skillet-grilled, which is my favorite.

Skillet-Grilled Parsnips

4 large fresh parsnips
1 tablespoon vegetable oil
salt and pepper to taste
1 tablespoon unsalted butter or margarine

1. Trim off the tops; wash and peel the parsnips. Trim off any stem that might be a little woody. Slice the parsnips lengthwise into $1/4$-inch-thick strips.

2. Heat the oil in a large skillet and fry the parsnip strips over medium heat until they are tender and lightly browned.

3. Add the butter or margarine and melt. Sprinkle on the salt and pepper and toss the parsnips to coat with the butter and seasonings.

Serves 4 as a side dish

Week Twenty-nine (MID-SEPTEMBER TO HARD FROST) *Harvest pumpkins; put your garden away for the winter.*

Not long after Labor Day, the nights begin to cool, and your garden production slows down. You have eaten the peas, lettuce, radishes, beets, squash, and melons by now, so remove all their vines and remains and put them in the compost pile. Leave the corn stalks and runner beans in place so as not to disturb the pumpkins, which should be turning bright orange.

When the pumpkins are ripe, go ahead and start making pie filling with them. It freezes well and can be used for all the winter holidays. Think about making a harvest scene with your dried corn stalks bunched together and surrounded by pumpkins; then throw all the remains of those crops into the compost pile. The parsnips and Hamburg parsley can remain in the ground right up until the first snowfall.

After you have removed all the dead plants, cover the garden with a layer of leftover straw and compost; then add a layer of fallen leaves. Be sure to mark the rows of parsnips and parsley so that you can find them.

All of this mulch and organic matter will begin to decompose over the winter. You can dig it in next year when it is time to start your garden again for another season.

An Edible Landscape

Growing an Edible Landscape is really just a different way of looking at the yard around your home. Too often we forget that there are beautiful flowering trees and shrubs that can also provide us with great-tasting fruit to eat. We plant flower beds for their beauty and don't realize that many garden vegetables and herbs are also very attractive.

In England the yard around a home is called a garden. In this chapter I will show you ways of transforming your yard into a lovely garden that is not only beautiful to behold but also can provide you with wonderful things to eat.

For instance, instead of planting a forsythia bush, you can plant a blueberry bush, which is adorned with pale flowers in the spring, juicy berries in the summer, and colorful foliage in the fall. Instead of planting an ornamental pear or crab apple tree, you can plant a fruitful cherry or plum tree whose blossoms in the spring rival those of any flowering tree. Instead of a flower bed with petunias and salvia, you can plant a bed with edible nasturtiums, calendula, viola, and lettuce as pretty as any flower.

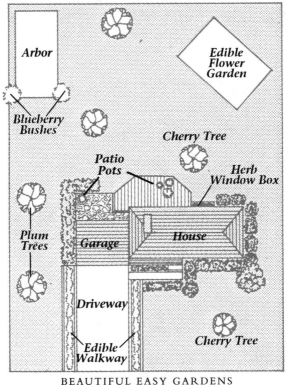

BEAUTIFUL EASY GARDENS

This edible garden is not a garden that is contained within a specific area. It is really a landscape composed of five different mini-gardens, including these:

- **An edible flower bed** with red and green leaf lettuce, nasturtium, viola, and calendula, which will make the most colorful flower bed and salad you've ever had
- **Patio pots and window boxes** with herbs, tomatoes, ornamental peppers—even eggplants—for your patio or rooftop garden
- **Arbors and arches** with grapes and Scarlet Runner beans growing up on trellises and canopies
- **Trees and shrubs** with blueberries, plums, and cherries being grown instead of the more common trees and shrubs of a typical landscape
- **Edible walkway borders** with Alpine strawberries, thyme, lavender, and rosemary growing as ground covers

This edible landscape garden is also one of the easiest to plant and maintain. You don't have to preorder any catalogs and wait for mail orders, you don't have to start and nurture any seedlings indoors, you can plant only the mini-gardens you feel you have room and time for, and you can easily buy everything you need at your local garden center when you have the time to do it.

If you do decide to plant a grape arbor, a fruit tree or two, and maybe a blueberry bush, don't expect to be able to harvest fruit from these plants the very first year. All these plants need at least two years to develop the strong root system needed to produce a lot of fruit in years to come. You can look forward to harvesting a few grapes and blueberries in the second year, but no real production until the third or even fourth year. It is rare for a plum or cherry tree, or any other fruit tree for that matter, to produce much fruit before the fourth year. Be patient and you will be rewarded.

A note on pest control: The fruits I suggest you grow in your edible landscape—Alpine strawberries, grapes, blueberries, plums, and cherries—are all very resistant to disease and pests. You should have no problems at all with the strawberries and the blueberries. The leaves and vines of grapes can become damaged by Japanese beetles. These are easily picked off by hand and then drowned in soapy water. You can also hang a Japanese beetle trap in the yard or spray the beetles with a prepared pyrethrum spray you can buy at your garden center. Please follow the manufacturer's instructions when using pyrethrum spray.

Neither plum nor cherry trees are highly susceptible to pest attack the way apple trees are. Prevention is the best cure, so I suggest spraying your trees with dormant oil spray, available in most garden centers, in the early spring before the buds open. An annual application of dormant oil will prevent most pests, such as codling moths or plum curculio, from attacking your trees. If you feel you need more information about specific tree pests in your area, please ask your local cooperative extension office to diagnose the problem and offer a nonchemical cure.

Instead of following a weekly calendar of gardening work activities, this plan will cover each mini-garden by the seasons. Most of the activity takes place in April, May, and June, when all of the planting is done, but the rewards carry on into June, July, August, and September, when the fruits of your labor move onto the table.

An Edible Flower Bed

Almost everyone has a small strip of ground tucked in between the driveway and the house or along the front or back of his or her property that is the perfect size for an edible flower bed. All you need is an area approximately 8 to 10 feet long and 3 to 4 feet wide that receives six to eight hours of direct sunlight each day. You are going to plant colorful and graceful red and green leaf lettuce; nasturtiums, whose leaves taste like watercress and whose flowers are bright and tasty, too; bushy calendula, whose flower petals add spice to a salad; and dainty violas, whose flowers add color and a little bit of tang.

For this garden you will need to buy the following supplies:

- one 40-pound bag of compost or organic humus and one 4-cubic-foot bag of sphagnum peat moss, which you will dig into the soil to enrich it and make it easier to work with
- one 40-pound bag of shredded pine bark or pine needles or another bag of peat moss for mulch
- one $2^1/_2$- to 5-pound box of blended natural organic fertilizer
  one packet each of nasturtium, calendula, red leaf lettuce, and green leaf lettuce
- one six-pack of viola transplants

All the flowers you will grow in this patch prefer to be planted in spring-time, when the weather is still a little cool. In the early spring, as soon as the ground can be worked, dig up your edible flower bed. I suggest digging an area 8 to 10 feet long and 3 to 4 feet wide. Many of us have this type of patch along the house under a window or along a fence in the yard. Be sure that the area receives six to eight hours or more of direct sunlight each day.

Dig up the area with a forked spade and break up all the clumps. Add the compost, peat moss, and 2 cups of balanced natural organic fertilizer to the soil and dig the soil again to incorporate the organic matter. Rake the area smooth, and you are ready to plant.

Plant the nasturtiums along the front of the garden 6 inches in from the edge. Simply poke the seeds down into the ground 1 inch deep with your finger. Cover with soil, firm down, and water.

Along the back of the garden, 4 inches in from the edge, plant a row of calendula, which are 16- to 18-inch tall bushy plants with yellow blossoms. Dig a trench $1/2$ inch deep and sprinkle in the seeds spaced 4 inches apart. Cover with soil, firm down with your hand, and water.

Mark a 2-foot by 2-foot area in the middle of the garden and transplant the violas spaced equally apart. They will grow and fill in this entire area. Dig a small hole for each viola. Remove the plant from the container, place the root ball in the hole, gather the soil up around it, firm down, and water.

Plant the lettuce in the remaining areas of the garden. Instead of planting the seeds in rows, scatter them over the soil in the areas that haven't been planted, leaving 6 to 8 inches on either side for the nasturtiums and calendu-la. Plant one packet of red leaf lettuce on one side and one packet of green leaf lettuce on the other side of the violas. Cover the lettuce seeds lightly with soil, firm down the area with your hand, and water.

Keep the seeds watered carefully until they germinate in a week to ten days. Keep the soil moist but not soggy. Once the seeds germinate, you can start to thin the lettuce and begin using the leaves in salads.

Edible Flower Salad

Most people know how to make a salad, but with flowers? It's really quite simple. Gather the red and green lettuce leaves, a few nasturtium leaves, and any other salad greens you have. Nibble on a nasturtium leaf. It tastes slightly like watercress. Wash and dry all the greens thoroughly. Place the salad greens in a bowl and toss them together.

Pick one golden calendula flower and separate the petals. Sprinkle a few petals on the salad greens. Pick a few nasturtium flowers and viola flowers. Scatter them over the greens for accent and color. Dress the salad with your favorite light dressing and serve. It is best if you take the first bite and prove to your skeptical friends that these flowers and greens are good to eat.

Patio Pots and Window Boxes

Most people like to place pots of flowering plants along the edges of their patio or deck to add color and to create a roomlike atmosphere. Window boxes are also making a return as people try to adorn the outside of their homes.

But there is no reason on earth why you should think that the only option is to fill these containers with petunias, geraniums, and other common flowers. No! You can fill your window boxes with miniature basil plants or parsley, sage, rosemary, and thyme. Patio pots can hold bushy green pepper plants with bright red pods, blue-green eggplants with violet-hued blossoms; even a tomato plant flanked by four mini-basil plants would look great on your patio, deck, or balcony garden. Imagine serving a lunch alfresco on the patio and picking a tomato right off the vine not 2 feet away and slicing it for your guests. Wouldn't that be great? Here's how to do it.

Herb Window Box

Fill a window box with good-quality potting soil. Add 2 to 3 cups of compost or organic humus and $1/2$ cup of natural organic fertilizer blended for vegetables. Stir the soil, compost, and fertilizer to blend well.

Buy one small pot each of parsley, sage, rosemary, and thyme. Water the plants until the soil is good and soggy. Dig four evenly spaced holes in the window-box soil slightly larger and deeper than the root balls of the plants. Place the plants into the holes slightly deeper than they were in their pots, gather the soil around their stems, firm down with your hand, and water. Attach the window box to a window that gets at least six to eight hours of full sun every day. Water the window box at least once a week unless you have adequate rain. You want the soil to be moist but not soggy. Sprinkle 2 tablespoons of fertilizer in the window box each month and start picking the leaves of the herbs in about two weeks. If you go away for vacation during the summer, these herbs may start to send up flowers and bloom. You can leave them in bloom for their attractiveness or pinch off the blooms and continue harvesting the herbs for cooking.

You can plant other window boxes with other herbs such as miniature basil, Corsican mint, chives, or lavender. All these herbs are commonly available at garden centers, and they grow short and compact rather than tall and lanky, like dill. You can easily transfer the window-box idea to long, narrow planters that can ring your patio or rest on the railing of your deck.

Spreadable Herb Cheese

This is a recipe for a spreadable cream cheese spiked with garlic and your own fresh herbs. Place a mound of herbed cheese in the center of a platter and surround with crackers, fresh fruit, and tiny knives for serving.

> *1 8-ounce package of cream cheese*
> *1/2 cup milk*
> *1/2 teaspoon fresh garlic, minced*
> *1/4 cup finely minced fresh parsley, sage, rosemary, thyme, and chives or a combination of herbs of your choice*
> *salt and pepper to taste*

1. Allow the cheese to warm to room temperature. Place the cheese, milk, garlic, minced herbs, salt, and pepper in a food processor. Pulse a few times to form a creamy paste. Add more milk if you feel the cheese is not yet as spreadable as you prefer.

2. Scoop the cheese into a bowl, cover, and refrigerate for at least two hours or overnight. Before serving, warm the cheese to room temperature. Place the cheese on a platter with the crackers and fruit and serve with wine.

Serves 4 to 8 as snacks

Cream of Vegetable Soup with Herbs

1 tablespoon unsalted butter or margarine
1 small onion, chopped
2 medium white potatoes, chopped
1 carrot, peeled and chopped
1 small zucchini, chopped
1 quart chicken stock or broth
¼ cup minced fresh window-box herbs
salt and pepper to taste
1 pint half-and-half

1. Melt the butter or margarine in a large soup pot over medium heat. Add the onion, potatoes, carrot, and zucchini and fry for five minutes, stirring often.

2. Add the chicken stock and the herbs and raise to a boil. Reduce the heat to medium-low and simmer, covered, for twenty minutes.

3. Place the soup in a food processor and pulse to form a creamy soup. Return the soup to the pot. Add the salt, pepper, and half-and-half and heat for fifteen minutes, but do not boil. Stir often.

4. Serve hot or cold with a dollop of sour cream in the middle and a few fresh, minced herbs on top.

Serves 4 to 6

Planting Pots

A lot of people have planters that measure at least 2 feet by 2 feet and 2 feet high. Garden centers carry a wide assortment of large planters, and you can often find them at yard sales. Instead of putting bushes in them, try planting a tomato plant, an eggplant, or an ornamental pepper plant. Plant them all in the same way.

Fill the planter with potting soil. Add a gallon of compost or organic humus and a cup of natural organic fertilizer. Stir the soil, humus, and fertilizer to blend well. Buy one large plant—either tomato, ornamental pepper, or eggplant—at your garden center. Soak the soil in the pot. Dig a hole slightly larger than the root ball of the plant. Place the plant into the hole slightly deeper than it was in the pot, gather the soil up around the stem, firm down with your hands, and water. Your tomato plant will need support as it grows, so drive a 1-inch-thick wooden stake into the soil 6 inches from the tomato plant stem. As the tomato grows, tie the stem to the stake with twine or string. Eggplant and pepper plants are sturdy enough to grow without support stakes. Plant four mini-basils in the pot with the tomato, and you have the makings of a simple summer salad or pasta dish.

As with the window boxes or other planting pots, you will need to water your large planter weekly during the hot summer months. Water until the soil is damp but not soggy. Add 2 tablespoons fertilizer to the pot each month.

You can pick the peppers at their immature green stage or let them ripen to a bright red color. Either way you can chop them for use in salsa or other Mexican dishes, just like fresh jalapeño peppers, which also make a nice potted plant.

Be sure to choose the tiny Italian or Japanese eggplant varieties. They are more attractive than the full-sized eggplants you see in the market. Pick the eggplants when they are purple and use them to make ratatouille, baba ghanoush, or eggplant Parmesan.

Arbors and Arches

Many homes have trellises, arbors, and arches that support clematis, roses, wisteria, and morning glory. I suggest that you plant annual Scarlet Runner beans and perennial grapevines instead.

Scarlet Runner beans have been handed down to modern growers by Native American gardeners. They are vigorous growers with long tendrillike vines bearing bright scarlet flowers that later give way to long, tasty green beans that can be eaten fresh or dried. Scarlet Runner bean blossoms also attract hummingbirds.

I'll never forget my home in Spain, where grapevines crawled over our patio canopy and provided cooling shade and delicious fruit during the summer. Grapevines will last for years once you get them started. Here's how.

Grapevines or runner beans will grow on any trellis or arbor strong enough to hold a climbing rose bush. You can buy arched arbors at garden centers or through catalogs. The posts at the corner of an open porch will also provide good support. In any case build or install the trellis or arbor of your choice.

Grapes

For grapes, plant one vine at the base of each side of an arched trellis or at the base of the two front posts holding up your patio canopy. For a freestanding gazebo plant four grapevines at equal spaces around the structure.

Most well-stocked garden centers will carry a selection of seedless grape varieties. You can also order from any of these three catalogs:

- Miller Nurseries, West Lake Road, Canandaigua, NY 14424; (800) 836–9630
- Northwoods Nursery, 28696 South Cramer, Molalla, OR 97038; (503) 651–3737
- Stark Bros., Box 10, Louisiana, MO 63353–0010; (800) 325–4180

Buy as many grapevines as you need from this list of seedless varieties; Candace, Himrod, Seedless Concord.

At the base of each post or arch, dig a hole slightly larger and deeper than the roots. Add a shovelful of compost or other organic matter to the hole and stir the soil around. Place the vine into the hole at the same depth as the vine was planted at the nursery. You can see the spot by looking at the root of the vine. Fill the hole with soil, firm down with your hand, and water. Place a layer of mulch—compost, shredded leaves or bark, or your favorite—12 inches all around the vine. Water it once a week during the first year and train the vine to grow up on the trellis by attaching it with a piece of soft string.

Grape Jam

You won't be able to harvest any grapes until the second or third season. When you do, you will probably eat most of your delicious grapes by just popping them into your mouth. But if you plant Seedless Concord grapes, they make a wonderful jam just like grandmother used to make.

4 pounds seedless grapes (approximately 1 gallon)
1 cup water
8 cups sugar
6 half-pint jars
paraffin wax

1. Wash the grapes and remove any stems. Place them in a large kettle, bring to a boil, and turn the heat to low. Cover and simmer for one hour, stirring often. Grapes are very juicy, and they usually provide their own juice for cooking, but you may have to add a little bit of water to keep them from sticking.

2. Add the sugar and continue to cook another hour or until the jam is thick. Stir often and be patient.

3. Pour the jam into the jars and seal with paraffin wax according to package instructions.

Makes 6 half-pint jars

Runner Beans

Planting the runner beans is very similar. Purchase Scarlett Runner beans, which are widely available in seed packets at most garden centers. Wait until the soil is thoroughly warm and all danger of frost has passed in your area. Dig the soil around the base of your trellis, patio post, or gazebo to a depth of 6 inches. Work a few shovelfuls of organic matter into the soil and rake it smooth. Plant the seeds by poking them down into the soil to a depth of 1 inch spaced 6 inches apart. Cover with soil, firm down, and water. Keep the seeds watered until they germinate. Place a 4-inch layer of mulch on the soil around the beans after they have sprouted and started to grow.

Scarlet Runner Bean Salad

1 pound Scarlet Runner beans
1 tablespoon red wine vinegar
1 teaspoon Dijon mustard
1 tablespoon minced fresh herbs such as parsley, chives, or thyme
salt and pepper to taste
3 tablespoons olive or other salad oil

1. Wash the beans and trim off the stems. Place them in a pan of water and boil for five to eight minutes until tender crisp. Drain the beans and cool them in cold water.

2. Make the dressing by stirring together the vinegar, mustard, herbs, salt, and pepper to taste. Add the olive oil a few drops at a time and whisk to form a creamy dressing.

3. Place the beans lengthwise on a plate. Drizzle the dressing over and serve.

Serves 4

Trees and Shrubs

Lovely spring-blooming ornamental trees increase the value of your home and provide you with beauty. Cherry and plum are two of the most beautiful ornamental trees in the world, and they also provide you with abundant fruit for eating. The same can be said for blueberry bushes, which can easily take the place of forsythia, mock orange, lilac, or any other strictly ornamental bush.

Because both cherry and damson plum trees grow only 10 to 12 feet tall and 6 to 8 feet wide, almost any yard has room to plant both of them. If you only have room for one, you make the call. Of course you could always have two cherry trees and two plum trees if you like. A blueberry bush grows slowly but eventually achieves a height of 6 to 8 feet and a width of 4 feet over a period of years.

For bright-red, sour pie cherries, select one North Star cherry tree. If you prefer dark-red, sweet cherries, choose one dwarf Stella. Both are self-pollinating.

Select one damson plum tree, which is also self-pollinating.

Select two blueberry bushes such as New Jersey, Early Blue, or Patriot. You must grow more than one blueberry bush in order for it to pollinate and set fruit.

Fruit Trees

In early spring set the trees with their burlapped roots out in the yard along a fence row or any place you would put an ornamental tree. The spots you choose to plant the trees should get full sun for eight to ten hours a day. For each tree you are planting, dig a hole in the ground twice as wide and slightly deeper than the root ball of the tree. Remove the plastic wrap but not the burlap wrap around the tree's root ball. Place the tree in the hole so that it rests at the same depth it was when it was at the nursery. Look at the trunk to see the soil line on the bark. Scoop two shovels full of compost or peat moss into the hole and start adding the soil back to the hole. When it is half full, firm down the soil with your hand or boot. Fill the hole with soil and place a 2- to 4-inch layer of mulch around the tree. Leave 2 inches between the tree trunk and the mulch. Slowly pour two watering cans full of water onto the soil, letting the water seep in each time.

Your cherry tree will not bear much fruit until the third or fourth year, but then you can enjoy cherries in this simple recipe.

Cherry Muffins

³/₄ cup sweet or sour cherries, pitted and chopped

1 egg, beaten

1 cup milk or buttermilk

3 tablespoons melted unsalted butter or margarine

2 cups sifted flour

3 teaspoons baking powder

¹/₂ teaspoon salt

3 tablespoons sugar

1. Preheat the oven to 400 degrees F. Grease a muffin tin.

2. Place the pitted cherries, beaten egg, milk, and butter in a mixing bowl and stir to blend well.

3. Place the flour, baking powder, salt, and sugar in another bowl and stir to blend well. Pour the wet ingredients over the dry ingredients and stir quickly and lightly, just enough to make a wet dough.

4. Place the dough into the muffin tin and bake for fifteen to twenty minutes. Remove from the tin and serve.

Makes 1 dozen muffins

Damson Plum Pie

4 cups damson plums, pitted and chopped

1¹/₂ cups sugar

2 tablespoons flour

¹/₄ teaspoon salt

1 prepared pie crust (enough for a top and bottom crust)

1 tablespoon butter

¹/₄ cup milk

1. Preheat the oven to 450 degrees F.

2. Place the plums in a medium mixing bowl and cover with sugar, flour, and salt. Stir to blend well.

3. Line a 9-inch pie pan with crust. Place the plum mixture on the crust. Top with remaining crust either as one crust or cut it into strips and arrange a lattice-crust topping. Brush the top crust with milk.

4. Bake for ten minutes, reduce heat to 350 degrees F., and bake twenty to thirty minutes longer or until pie is golden brown.

Makes 1 pie

Blueberry Bushes

Plant the blueberries in much the same way as you planted the trees. In early spring select the sites for your two blueberry bushes, making sure they will get at least six hours of full sun each day. Blueberries make nice bushes around doorways and on the edge of patios.

Dig two holes slightly deeper and wider than the root balls of the blueberry bushes. Dig a shovelful of compost or peat moss into each hole and place each bush in the hole at the same depth as it was at the nursery. Look for the soil line on the stem. Fill the hole with soil and firm down. Slowly pour two 2- to 3-gallon watering cans full of water on each bush, letting the water soak in each time. Place a layer of peat moss or sawdust mulch around each bush and water weekly during the first year. Next spring add a cupful of natural organic fertilizer (one that is formulated for acid-loving plants) around each bush and add another layer of mulch to stifle weeds and conserve water.

You might be able to harvest a few blueberries in the second year, but after that you should have enough berries for this and many other recipes.

Blueberry Cake

1 cup fresh blueberries
¹/₄ cup unsalted butter or margarine at room temperature
1¹/₃ cups all-purpose flour
2 teaspoons baking powder
¹/₄ teaspoon salt
1 cup sugar
1 egg, beaten
¹/₂ teaspoon vanilla
¹/₂ cup milk

1. Preheat the oven to 350 degrees F. and butter a 9-inch-square cake pan.

2. Wash the berries and remove any stems. Place them in a bowl and cover with ¹/₄ cup sugar.

3. In a large bowl mix together the butter, flour, baking powder, salt, and sugar. Add the egg, vanilla, and milk and beat until smooth.

4. Pour the batter into the baking pan and scatter the blueberries on top. Place in the oven and bake for twenty-five to thirty minutes.

Makes nine 3-inch squares

Edible Walkway Borders

Almost everybody has some kind of walkway along a driveway or a sidewalk, by a fence, or along a road. Instead of planting the usual spreading yews or pachysandra ground covers, think about planting hardy herbs such as lavender, thyme, or rosemary, which are low-growing shrubby herbs, or a bed of Alpine strawberries, which can form an attractive ground cover dotted with luscious, tiny strawberries.

In early spring, as soon as the ground can be worked, dig along the edge of your walkway or other chosen site with a forked spade or small rotary tiller. Dig a patch 2 feet wide and as long as you want it to be. Work 2 or 3 bushels or bags of compost or shredded leaves or other organic material into the soil by digging and turning the soil with a spade. Break up any clumps and rake the area smooth.

You now need to buy as many rosemary, thyme, Alpine strawberries, or lavender bedding plants as it takes to fill this area. All these plants will bush out and grow much larger than they are now. If your walkway is 10 feet long and 2 feet wide, you need to buy six transplants.

Set the transplants 18 inches apart in the row. Dig a hole slightly larger and deeper than the root ball of the transplant. Place the plant in the hole and gather the soil up 2 to 4 inches around the stem. Firm the soil down with your hands and water well.

Mulch the entire row with peat moss, shredded bark, or whatever mulch material you find attractive. The mulch will stifle weeds and conserve water.

All these plants grow well under dry droughtlike conditions, but be sure to water them weekly during their first year of growth. Simply pour a watering can full of water over them once a week. Spray hoses tend to deliver too much water at one time and too much is lost. Once the plants get established, you can reduce their watering to once a month.

You can start to harvest the herbs in a month's time. Give them time to get established; then start snipping leaves off here and there. Thyme, lavender, and strawberries are perennial in all parts of the country, whereas rosemary is perennial only in warmer areas.

Harvest the thyme and rosemary any time the plant is established by snipping off leaves. You can use them fresh in cooking or dry them for winter use. Next summer the lavender will shoot up long sprigs of blue flowers, which you can harvest for a fragrant potpourri. You really should not harvest Alpine strawberries the first year; pull off the flowers before the plant sets fruit (this allows more energy to go into strong root production) and let the plant establish itself for prolonged growth and higher strawberry yield over the years. Alpine strawberries are perennial, and they do not send out shoots like other strawberries, which makes them attractive for a landscape.

A Cottage Orchard

A small orchard of a few fruit trees, berry bushes and brambles, and a grape arbor is one of the prettiest sights to behold in the springtime, when all their delicate flowers are in full bloom. A Cottage Orchard is quite a bit larger than the other gardens described in this book, measuring 50 feet by 30 feet, but you don't have to plant everything that is suggested. You can plant one cherry tree or a grape arbor and have your own private little orchard.

Growing this garden takes a bit of patience. Although the raspberries will produce fruit in the second year, the grapes and blueberries won't produce much until the third year, and the trees often take as long as four years before they bear fruit. Once you get the orchard established, however, your biggest problem will be what to do with all the fruit, and your orchard will last for twenty to thirty years, with very low maintenance.

How can an orchard be easy to maintain? First, the orchard is small—only six fruit trees, all of which are dwarf varieties that will only grow 10 to

12 feet tall. There is minimal pruning involved with dwarf trees, and the ones I have suggested are the new, improved disease-resistant varieties, which are rapidly coming onto the market. Insect pests can be controlled with a light spraying program that won't take up much of your time and won't harm your health or the environment.

Your cottage orchard will include two apple trees, two plum trees, and two cherry trees—one sweet cheery and one sour or pie cherry. You will have two blueberry bushes, two grapevines trained on an arbor, and a patch of red raspberry canes.

Instead of giving you a weekly work schedule as I did in many of the other chapters in this book, I am giving you a three-year seasonal work schedule, because an orchard takes three years to come to fruition, as opposed to a vegetable garden, which is an annual event. The first year will be dedicated to designing, planting, and protecting your young orchard from harsh weather and varmints. The second year will be spent on pest control, mulching and mowing, and light pruning. You will get to enjoy raspberries in the second year and possibly a blueberry or two. The third year will focus on harvesting and cooking your wonderful fruit as well as continuing a light maintenance program.

Everyone is probably well aware of the environmental benefits of planting trees. Trees fight air pollution by consuming carbon dioxide and releasing oxygen. An orchard can also be your own mini wildlife center or refuge. Bees will fill your orchard with buzzing in spring, when they pollinate the fruit flowers. You might think about building a beehive with your kids to attract even more bees and provide yourself with honey. Birds will come to your orchard to eat bugs right off the tree trunks and to find shelter for their nests. Finally, you could build a little bench or area in the orchard where you and your family can go for picnics.

The Three-Year Seasonal Guide

In the first year you will design and build your orchard and choose, plant, and care for your young trees, bushes, and vines.

Year One (WINTER) *Select and buy your orchard plants.*

It really is a toss-up whether you should buy your orchard plants from a mail-order catalog or from your local garden center or nursery. Catalogs give you the joy of leafing through their colorful pages and reading about the different fruits you will soon plant. A garden center will be able to give you personal service and advice, and you will be able to see the actual trees and other fruit stock you are buying.

The only major difference is that a garden center will likely sell you a balled-root tree, that is, the roots of the tree will be encased in soil and wrapped in burlap, whereas a catalog company will send you what are known as bare-root trees; that is, they won't have soil or burlap around the root. A bare-root tree is dormant, making it easier for shipping. A balled-root tree has already leafed out, making it more attractive to the buyer at a garden center. Both methods of presentation provide excellent-quality trees.

The key to buying fruit trees and plants is the guarantee. I've never heard of a catalog company or a reputable garden center that wouldn't guarantee the quality of its product and offer to replace it free of charge if the plant should fail. A fruit tree can cost more than $25 and a blueberry bush as much as $50. You are investing quite a bit of money in your orchard, so you want to be sure whoever you buy from stands behind the product. Always ask for a guarantee, just in case.

Order any or all of these catalogs:

- Gurney's Seed & Nursery Co., 110 Capital Street, Yankton, SD 57079. Colorful flower and vegetable catalog with a nice selection of fruits at good prices.
- Henry Field's Seed and Nursery Co., 415 North Burnett, Shenandoah, IA 51602; (605) 665–9391. General flower and vegetable catalog with a good selection of fruits at good prices.
- Miller Nurseries, West Lake Road, Canandaigua, NY 14424; (800) 836–9630. Large selection of fruits and ornamental trees and bushes, too.
- Northwoods Nursery, 28696 South Cramer Road, Molalla, OR 97038; (503) 651–3737. Informative catalog with an emphasis on fruits; good for the Pacific Northwest and the North in general.

• Stark Bros., Box 10, Louisiana, MO 63353–0010; (800) 325–4180. Stark's has been in business since 1816. The first tree I ever planted was a Montmorency cherry from Stark's.

Many fruit-tree catalogs, and often a garden center, will sell trees that are already pruned. They are sometimes called "deluxe" or "premium." This is the most important pruning your tree will ever get, so I suggest that you invest the few extra dollars and let the experts prune your tree for you before you plant it.

I haven't suggested that you plant either peaches or pears in your orchard. Peaches are a little bit difficult to grow because they are very sensitive to cold temperatures. If you really love peaches and want to grow them, consult with your local cooperative extension office or garden center for their advice on whether you can grow peaches where you live and what varieties are best for your area. I didn't include pears because I was running out of room to plant and because I wanted a fruit tree to bear fruit for you in early summer. If you prefer pears, grow them if you like. Here's what I suggest you buy:

• Apple trees: Apple trees are one of the most disease-prone trees you can plant, but breeders have developed new varieties of apples that are immune to disease and still have good flavor. I am particularly fond of yellow or golden apples, but if you are not, feel free to buy two red apple trees. Here are my suggestions:

> One dwarf disease-resistant red apple tree: Jonafree, Liberty, Freedom, MacFree, or Akane
>
> and
>
> One dwarf disease-resistant golden apple tree: Grimes or Golden Delicious

• Cherry trees: Cherry trees are fairly disease- and pest-resistant, and they require very little spraying or pruning. Your biggest problem will be keeping the birds away from the fruit when it gets ripe. Choose:

> One North Star cherry tree: North Star is a naturally dwarf tree that grows only 10 feet tall. It is naturally self-pollinating and produces tart cherries that make great pies and preserves.
>
> and

One Stella dwarf cherry tree: Stella is the one self-pollinating cherry tree that bears dark-red sweet cherries that are ready to eat right off the tree.

- Plum trees: Plum trees are considered the easiest trees to grow for the Cottage Orchard. They bloom beautifully, they grow to a naturally compact shape, and they are not bothered by too many pests or diseases. The vast majority of plum trees are members of either the European or Japanese family. The Japanese plums are the ones you usually find in the supermarket in July. They prefer to grow in the warmer climates, wherever peaches grow well; they are considered the best ones for eating fresh out of hand; and they tend to begin bearing fruit in as little as three years. European plums prefer colder climates; they make great jams but are also sweet right off the tree; and they tend to bear fruit in four years. In order to pollinate, however, Japanese plums need another Japanese plum nearby, so you have to plant two Japanese plums or two European plums, not one from either family. Here are my suggestions:

  One European Blue Damson or Stanley Prune plum: Both varieties produce beautiful purple fruit with golden flesh; great for fresh eating and wonderful for jams and preserves; self-pollinating.

  and

  One European Green Gage plum; produces yellowish-green fruit great for eating fresh; prefers colder weather

  or

  Two Japanese plums: Shiro, Santa Rosa, Redheart, Ozark Premier, Superior, or Burbank

- Blueberries: Buy two different ones for good pollination. Buy one early variety such as Earliblue, Bluetta, or Patriot, and a later variety such as Jersey, Northblue, or Bluecrop.

- Grapes: Buy two seedless grapevines of your choice and of any color, either Red Candace, Reliance, or Vanessa (all red varieties); White Himrod, Interlaken, or Niagara (all white varieties); or Purple Glenora or Seedless Concord (both purple).

- Raspberries: The raspberry patch in the Cottage Orchard is designed to be 30 feet long, which will produce about 30 quarts of berries each year. Berries need to be planted 3 feet apart. If you want to reduce the size of your patch, reduce the size of your order accordingly.

Buy ten plants of virus-free Red Latham, Titan, Taylor, or Chilliwack.

Year One (LATE WINTER) *Design and build the orchard site.*

The Cottage Orchard is designed to be 50 feet long and 30 feet wide. Please refer to the diagram at the beginning of this chapter. The orchard I have envisioned has an ordered, formal feel to it. As you approach the orchard, you'll see the two blueberry bushes on either side of an 8-foot-tall grape arbor: then you pass through the arbor and proceed through your cherry, apple, and plum esplanade. The berry patch runs along the back of the orchard to form an outer boundary.

You don't have to conform to my design if the space around your home or site does not permit. You can break the design up and plant the berries along a fence, the blueberry bushes on either side of the back door, the grape arbor near the garage, and the trees wherever you can find the space. Just be sure to keep the apple trees and plum trees in sight of each other to ensure proper pollination. The cherry trees are self-pollinating and can be planted anywhere. All the trees will grow to be 10 to 12 feet tall and 6 to 8 feet wide, so give them room to grow. Once you have designed your area, place markers in the spots where you are going to plant the fruit trees, bushes, vines, and berries.

Year One (SPRING) *Plant your cottage orchard.*

Getting Ready

All your fruit plants need to be put in the ground as soon as they arrive. Leaving them out of the ground for even a few days can damage them quite severely. All of them need to be planted in early spring as soon as the ground in your area can be dug up with a shovel or a rotary tiller. Early spring can be anytime from March in Charlotte, St. Louis, and San Francisco to May in Denver, Minneapolis, or Buffalo. Ask the staff of your local garden center or your cooperative extension agent for the best time to plant in your area. But get ready, 'cause here they come.

You will need a short-handled, flat-blade digging spade to dig the planting holes for the trees, the grapevines, the raspberry canes, and the blueberry bushes. For the raspberry patch you need to dig a row 3 feet wide, 30 feet long, and 8 inches deep. You can do all this digging yourself with a forked spade, but you can also rent a rotary tiller for a day or hire a person to do the tilling for you.

Buy three 4-cubic-foot bags of sphagnum peat moss, two bags of compost or organic humus, and four bales of straw or four bags of shredded pine needles or bark for mulch. Work a little peat moss into each hole you dig for the trees and bushes and a lot into the berry patch. Work the compost into the berry patch and use the mulch to spread around everything you have planted.

Buy or build a grape arbor about 8 feet high and 5 feet across. Grape arbors made of wood or steel tubing are readily available through catalogs and at garden centers. These arbors are a bit expensive, often more than $100, but they are a charming addition to your cottage orchard.

Buy three rolls of paper tree wrap, a lightweight paper that you wrap around the young tree trunks to protect them from critters, bugs, and cold weather.

Planting

As soon as the ground can be worked, prepare the berry patch. Measure an area 30 feet long and 3 feet wide. Clear any grass or sod growing on this area. Dig the soil to a depth of 8 inches. Break up any clods and discard any rocks, sticks, or other debris. Spread two bags of compost (the equivalent of two bushels if you have access to homemade compost) and one bag of sphagnum peat moss over the area and dig that into the soil. Rake the area smooth, and you are ready to plant.

Plant the raspberry canes by setting them 3 feet apart in the center of the row. Dig a hole slightly larger and deeper than the roots. Place the canes in the hole 1 inch deeper than they were at the nursery (look for the difference in color on the cane down near where the roots start). Firm the soil up around the canes, cut them back to 6 inches in length, and water.

Plant the trees by setting them out at their respective places in the orchard. Dig a hole twice as wide and slightly deeper than the bare root or root ball. (Every tree that you order will come with detailed planting instructions.) Remove the plastic wrap but leave the burlap wrap if your tree has one. The burlap will disintegrate right in the hole. Place the tree down into the hole so that it is at the same depth it was at the nursery. Ask your garden center operator to show you the exact point on the tree. Most catalog companies also indicate the planting-depth spot on their trees.

Mix a shovelful of compost or peat moss with some of the dirt you dug out of the hole and return the mixture to the hole. Start filling in the hole with soil, making sure that you hold the tree straight up. When the hole is half full of dirt, firm the soil down. Continue to fill the hole and firm the soil down. With the extra dirt form a circular embankment, or levee, around your tree about 8 inches from the trunk. This forms a little moat that captures water and keeps it near the tree. Wrap the tree trunk with paper wrap.

Plant the blueberry bushes in much the same way as you did the trees. Dig a hole twice as wide and slightly deeper than the roots or root ball of the bush. Place the bush in the hole at the same level it was at the nursery. Work a shovelful of compost or peat moss in with the soil and fill in the hole, firming the soil all around. You don't need to dig a moat for blueberries as you did for the fruit trees, but it won't hurt if you do.

Plant the grapevines by first installing the arbor according to manufacturer's instructions. Basically you dig the soil on either end, sink the stakes into the ground, and firm up with soil. Plant one grapevine at either end of the arbor. Dig a hole a foot wide and a foot deep. Add a shovelful of compost or peat moss to the hole and place the root in the hole at the same depth it was at the nursery. Fill the hole with soil, firm down, and water.

Mulch all the plants you have just planted. Spread any leftover compost or peat moss around the blueberry bushes and grapevines. Then spread the straw or other mulch around the base of the trees, canes, bushes, and vines to conserve water and stifle weeds.

Remember to give all your plants a slow, deep watering after you have planted them. Each tree should get at least two 2- to 3-gallon watering cans full of water, and all other plants should get at least one watering can full. Take your time and add the water very slowly so that it seeps down deep into the root system.

Year One (SUMMER) *Water, mulch, and protect your orchard.*

In the fall, add an extra layer of mulch to protect the plants from the cold winter.

As spring continues and the rains come, you probably won't have to water your orchard. But as soon as the rains stop and the warm weather arrives, you should water your orchard once a week. Follow the same watering-can procedures as mentioned previously or run a hose out to the site (you may need an extension). Place the nozzle, or hose coupling, at the base of your plants and let the water trickle out for twenty minutes. Move to another plant and continue.

Keep the lawn area around your orchard mowed. Be careful not to hit any of the trees with the lawn mower.

Watch for any signs of gnawing damage by rodents or deer. If you find damage, replace the paper wrap with hard plastic collars (available at garden centers). Pull the mulch back away from the trunk or vine to a distance of at least 4 inches. Rodents often find mulch to be a great place to live and your tree a great piece of wood to gnaw on.

Add extra straw or other mulch if weeds pop up. As the grapevines start to grow, train them to climb up on the arbor. Gently nudge them along by tying them to the arbor with soft string.

Year One (FALL) *Mulch; water.*

Be sure to give your trees 2 to 3 gallons of water once a week during dry fall spells.

Year two will be a fairly quiet year in the Cottage Orchard. Although the raspberry canes will produce plenty of fruit, and the blueberry bushes may produce a few berries, the rest of your plants will be setting down roots and establishing themselves for fruit production next year or the year after. You will continue to care for your plants by pruning them and controlling pests.

Year Two (LATE WINTER TO EARLY SPRING) *Prune.*

Except for the raspberry canes, the vines, bushes, and trees in your orchard should not be heavily pruned in their second year. In late winter or very early spring, prune lightly before the trees begin to bud out. Be sure to use sharp pruning shears.

Apple, Plum, and Cherry Trees. Shape these trees so that each tree has a strong central upward growing branch flanked by several lateral or side branches. This method is called the modified central leader. You should not let the central leader grow too tall because you want to encourage sunlight to reach down into the center of the tree. You probably will not have to do too much pruning on these trees until the third year.

Blueberry Bushes. Blueberry bushes need only light pruning during their entire life and then only to remove any dead branches.

Grapevines. Prune the grapevines to grow one strong central vine up and over the trellis. You want grapevines to grow bushy but not wild. Each year in the late winter or early spring, before the buds begin to swell, prune out any wildly growing vines and try to keep fostering the growth of the one central vine and perhaps a few secondary vines.

Raspberries. Raspberry plants are composed of perennial crowns that every year send up new canes, which bear fruit in their second year. In early spring cut back all old or weak canes to ground level. Thin the canes to fifteen per 4 feet of row and trim them to stand 3 feet in height. (In the fall, after the canes have fruited, you will remove the canes that have fruited by cutting them off at ground level. You can tell which canes have fruited by seeing the remains of their berry clusters.)

Year Two (EARLY SPRING) *Control pests.*

Because you have planted disease-resistant trees and virus-free raspberries, you should not be bothered by diseases in your orchard, but you still might be bothered by a few insect pests. Here's what to do:

Fruit Trees

- Dormant oil spray: While your fruit trees are still dormant just before the buds open, spray them with a horticultural oil spray. This EPA-approved oil will cover the tree's surface, smother and control codling moth larvae, scale, red bugs, aphids, and other insects. Since your trees are still quite small, you probably won't have to buy a large spray apparatus. You can do a good job with a smaller hand sprayer. Please follow manufacturer's instructions for solution mixture and application.

- Pheromone lure traps and sticky ball traps: Traps scented with a pheromone lure will help you control fruit flies, codling moths, and apple maggots, the three main insect pests you will probably have to deal with. Pheromone lures are biological scents that lure the male insect, confuse his mating cycle, and then trap him. Although they do not control 100 percent of all bugs, they are very effective, and the EPA is keen on encouraging their use because they are totally nontoxic and environmentally safe to use.

- Hang one codling moth trap and one red sticky ball with apple-maggot lure in each apple tree. Hang one fruit-fly trap with lure in each cherry tree. Plum trees are naturally disease-resistant and don't need any traps (just dormant oil spray).

- It is important to install the pheromone lure traps early in the spring before the insects get a chance to damage your trees. Hang the traps on the same day you spray with dormant oil. Hang the red sticky ball in late May or early June. Please read package instructions carefully before doing anything.

Grapes and Raspberries

- Grapes, and sometimes raspberries, are damaged by Japanese beetles. You can battle Japanese beetles by picking them off the vines by hand and drowning them in a soapy water solution, by hanging Japanese-beetle traps in your yard, or by spraying the bugs with pyrethrum spray. Please follow manufacturer's instructions when using pyrethrum sprays.

In addition to products available at your local garden center, here are several good catalogs that offer environmentally friendly pest-control products:

- Gardener's Supply, 128 Intervale Road, Burlington, VT 05401. Good supply catalog with many pest products.

- Gardens Alive! 5100 Schenley Place, Lawrenceburg, IN 47025. Highly recommended for products and information.

- Harmony Farm Supply, P.O. Box 460, Grafton, CA 95444. Excellent selection of traps, lures, and predatory insects.

- Integrated Fertility Management, 333-B Ohme Garden Road, Wenatchee, WA 98801. From deep in the heart of apple country, this catalog specializes in orchard products.

Birds

Birds are a major problem with raspberries, cherries, and blueberries. They always seem to swarm and eat the fruit just two days before you are ready to pick it. Protect your fruit by draping fruit-tree netting, available through catalogs and from garden centers, over your cherry trees, blueberry bushes, and raspberry canes. Birds might also eat your grapes on occasion.

There are many new organic and environmentally friendly pest-control products coming on the market each year. Look for products such as Organic Fruit Tree Spray from Gardens Alive; this spray is a combination of pyrethrum, rotenone, copper, and sulfur that will control a wide spectrum of pests and diseases. These products are safe to use if you follow the instructions carefully, and they should help simplify environmental fruit-tree growing. *Warning!* Even though biological and botanical pesticides are generally safe to use, it is very important that you read and follow the package instructions carefully. Keep all pesticides away from children.

There are many less common types of pests and diseases that can attack and damage your Cottage Orchard. If you have problems that you can't control, contact your cooperative extension office or garden center for help.

Year Two (LATE SPRING TO SUMMER) *Fertilize and keep up maintenance; water; harvest raspberries.*

In general your fruit trees will not benefit from added applications of fertilizer, but they will benefit from the addition of a few shovelfuls of compost or peat moss and another coating of mulch each year in the early spring. (After the trees are three to four years old, an annual application of a balanced natural organic fertilizer will be beneficial.)

Spread additional layers of compost, shredded leaves, or peat moss, plus another layer of mulch on your raspberry patch each year in early spring.

Add 1 cup of balanced natural organic fertilizer at the base of each grapevine each year, along with a shovelful of compost or peat moss and another layer of mulch.

Blueberries benefit from an annual application of natural organic fertilizer formulated for acid-loving plants such as azaleas. Apply the amount specified on the package instructions. One of the best mulches for blueberries is sawdust, which you can get at your local lumber mill or hardware store.

Remember that your plants are still young and you may need to water them occasionally during the dry summer months. Do water them weekly if your area is suffering from drought.

You will get a nice crop of raspberries in the second year. You probably will eat them as fast as you can pick them or simply put them in a bowl and pour cream over them. I've included a recipe in the Year Three section of this chapter in case you have an abundance and you want to try to cook with them.

Year Two (FALL) *Prune raspberries.*

After the raspberries have fruited, remove the canes that bore fruit by cutting them off at ground level. This makes room for new canes to shoot up next year to produce berries the following year. Shred the canes and add them to your compost pile.

During the third year the Cottage Orchard requires only light maintenance, so you can spend most of your time harvesting and cooking.

Year Three (LATE WINTER TO EARLY SPRING) *Prune trees and bushes.*

In year three your trees, and perhaps your blueberry bushes, will need a little light pruning. In the late winter or early spring, before the trees have started to bud, prune out any soft sucker branches that might have sprouted and trim off any dead branches or parts of limbs.

Year Three (SPRING AND SUMMER) *Continue maintaining your orchard.*

Remember to add compost and mulch every year to all your fruit plants and to add fertilizer to the grapes, blueberries, and raspberries. You may also add an application of balanced organic fertilizer to your trees this year. Read the manufacturer's instructions and sprinkle the correct amount in a circle around the tree on the ground below tips of the branches.

Probably in year three, and certainly in year four and for many more years to come, your Cottage Orchard will bear cherries and raspberries in late June and early July, blueberries in late July, grapes and plums in August, and apples in September. On the next few pages are some recipes to help you enjoy them.

Sour Cherry Cobbler

1¹/₂ cups sifted flour

2 teaspoons baking powder

¹/₂ teaspoon salt

¹/₂ cup sugar

¹/₄ cup unsalted butter or margarine

¹/₃ cup milk

1 egg, beaten

2 cups pitted sour cherries

1 tablespoon quick-cooking tapioca

1. Preheat the oven to 425 degrees F. Butter a shallow 1¹/₂-quart baking dish. Place the cherries in the dish, sprinkle with ¹/₄ cup sugar and the tapioca.

2. In a medium mixing bowl, combine the flour, baking powder, salt and ¹/₄ cup sugar. Stir to blend well.

3. Cut the butter into small chunks and work it into the flour mixture until the mixture resembles tiny nuggets. Add the milk to the flour mixture and stir until the dough is just wet.

4. Drop spoonfuls of dough on top of the cherries and bake in the oven for thirty minutes or until crust is light brown and cherries are bubbling. Let cool and serve.

Serves 4 to 6

Raspberry Flummery

A flummery is an old-fashioned dish of cooked berries swirled with whipped cream.

4 cups fresh raspberries

1 cup sugar

1 tablespoon cornstarch

¹/₄ cup water

1 cup heavy cream

1. Place the raspberries and sugar in a saucepan and cook over medium heat for fifteen minutes.

2. Mix the cornstarch and water in a small glass and pour into the hot berry mixture. Stir and cook until thickened. Remove from the heat and let cool.

3. Whip the heavy cream until stiff and fold into the cool berry mixture.

Serves 4 to 6

Blueberry Pie

4 cups blueberries
1¹/₄ cups sugar
1¹/₂ tablespoon cornstarch
1 prepared two-crust piecrust
1 tablespoon butter
¹/₄ cup milk

1. Preheat the oven to 450 degrees F. Line a 9-inch pie pan with one of the prepared pie crusts.

2. Place the blueberries in a large mixing bowl and sprinkle with the sugar and cornstarch. Stir to blend well.

3. Pour the blueberry mixture into the pie shell and dot with butter. Place the other crust on top as is or cut it into thin strips and arrange a lattice crust with the strips. Pinch and flute the piecrust edges. Brush the crust with milk.

4. Bake the pie at 450 degrees F. for ten minutes; then reduce heat to 350 degrees F. and bake twenty-five minutes longer.

Makes one 9-inch pie

Waldorf Salad with Grapes

2 cups grapes
1 cup diced apples
1 cup minced celery
1/2 cup chopped walnuts
1 cup light mayonnaise
lettuce leaves

1. Combine the grapes, apples, celery, and nuts in a large mixing bowl. Add the mayonnaise and stir to blend well.

2. Place lettuce leaves on individual plates and spoon mounds of salad onto each plate.

Serves 4 to 6

Plum Preserves

Damson, Green Gage, or Prune plums are known to make the best jam, but Japanese plums work well, too.

4 quarts fresh plums, pitted
4 cups water
8 to 10 cups sugar

1. Pit the fruit and cut it into small chunks. Add it to a large pot along with the water and the sugar.

2. Bring the mixture to a boil; then reduce the heat to medium and simmer, stirring often, until the plum preserve thickens.

3. Sterilize eight half-pint canning jars. Pour the hot plum preserve into the jars and coat with paraffin to seal.

Makes 8 half pints of plum preserves

Apple Brown Betty

2 cups fresh, unseasoned bread crumbs
¼ cup melted unsalted butter
4 cups apples, sliced
½ cup light brown sugar
¼ teaspoon ground nutmeg or mace
½ teaspoon ground cinnamon
juice and grated rind of ½ lemon

1. Preheat the oven to 350 degrees F. Butter a 1½-quart baking dish.

2. Make fresh bread crumbs by breaking day-old French bread or rolls into small pieces. Place the pieces in a food processor and process until crumbs form. Mix the bread crumbs with the butter in a medium mixing bowl and stir to blend well.

3. Make the sugar mixture by mixing together the sugar, nutmeg or mace, cinnamon, and lemon. Stir.

4. Place a layer of crumbs in the baking dish, top with half the apple slices and sprinkle with sugar mixture; add another layer of apples, then sugar mixture, and top with bread crumbs.

5. Cover the dish with foil and bake for twenty minutes. Remove the foil and bake another twenty minutes until the top is lightly browned.

Serves 4

Fruit Muffins

1 cup blueberries, pitted cherries, chopped apples, or raspberries
2 cups sifted flour
3 teaspoons baking powder
¹/₂ teaspoon salt
2 tablespoons sugar
1 egg, beaten
1 cup milk
3 tablespoons melted butter

1. Preheat the oven to 400 degrees F. Butter a muffin pan.

2. Place the fruit, flour, baking powder, salt, and sugar in a medium mixing bowl. Stir to blend well.

3. Place the egg, milk, and melted butter in a small mixing bowl. Stir to blend well. Add the wet ingredients to the dry ones and stir quickly to blend well. Don't overbeat.

4. Spoon the batter into the buttered muffin tin and bake at 400 degrees F. for fifteen minutes. Remove from the tin and cool.

Makes 12 muffins

There are hundreds of different ways to cook fruits in jams, preserves, cakes, compotes, pies, and other concoctions. Please go to your local library and check out a book on fruit cookery. Enjoy.

A Pan-Asian
Garden

*T*he Pan-Asian vegetable garden is the most exotic backyard garden described in this book. Most of us have eaten Chinese vegetables in restaurants, we've seen and cooked with a few from our supermarkets, and maybe some of us have been to Chinatown and learned even more about these foods, but not too many of us have seen these foods grown in a garden unless we live next door to an Asian family or in an Asian neighborhood. I tried to convince an editor of mine, Mei Mei Chan, that growing an Asian vegetable garden was a hot new food story when she politely informed me that she and her mother had always grown Chinese vegetables at their home in Chicago.*

I'm hooked on growing Asian vegetables, and I've learned some of their idiosyncracies and their names by growing a few different ones each year. Like most vegetables, they want lots of warm sun shining on a well-tilled soil that is rich in organic matter with a steady supply of fertilizer and moisture.

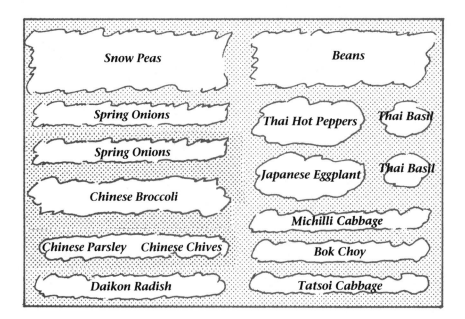

You are going to grow thirteen different types of vegetables in your 10-feet-wide-by-15-feet-long pan-Asian garden this year, including snow peas, long green spring onions, Chinese broccoli, chives and parsley, Japanese Daikon radishes, michilli cabbage, bok choy and flat-leaf tatsoi cabbage, yard-long green beans, Thai basil, Japanese eggplant, and incendiary Thai peppers.

Your garden will have four busy planting days beginning in early March when you start the basil, peppers, chives, and eggplant on a windowsill indoors; still cool early April when you plant peas, onions, broccoli, radishes, and parsley outdoors in the garden; early May when you plant cabbage, bok choy, and tatsoi in the garden; and June 1 when you plant peppers, eggplant, chives, basil, and beans in the garden. I suggest you add another planting day in August for a fall crop of cabbages that will last you until cold weather. There will also be one busy day when you dig up the garden and add the fertilizer and organic matter.

If you like Asian food, this will be a wonderful garden to plant and enjoy. You probably have plenty of your favorite stir-fry Oriental recipes, but I have added seven of my own that I hope you will try.

The Weekly Guide

Week One (FEBRUARY 1) *Order seed catalogs.*

Asian vegetable seeds are not as hard to obtain as they used to be. You will find a fairly good selection in a variety of all-around catalogs. But there are a few catalogs that carry an extensive listing of Asian seeds and some catalogs that specialize in Asian seeds only. Order as many of these catalogs as you like:

- The Good Earth Seed Company, P.O. Box 5644, Redwood City, CA 94063; (414) 364–4494. Very good Asian seed collection plus cookbooks, Asian sauces, and Chinese woks, cleavers, and other cooking utensils.
- Johnny's Selected Seeds, Foss Hill Road, Albion, ME 04910; (207) 437–4301. Well-rounded catalog with an excellent collection of Asian seeds plus reliable growing advice.

- Park Seed Co., Cokesbury Road, Greenwood, SC 29647. Great flower catalog; also has a very good selection of Asian seeds.
- Stokes Seeds Inc., Box 548, Buffalo, NY 14240; (416) 688–4300. Good all-around catalog with a fine selection of Asian seeds.
- Sunrise Enterprises, P.O. Box 330058, West Hartford, CT 06133. Catalog costs $2.00, which can be used as credit on your first order. Good selection of seeds as well as flowers, live plants, and cookbooks.

Week Two (MID-FEBRUARY) *Survey your friends and family.*

Almost everyone likes Chinese food, and more and more people are discovering Japanese and Thai food. I will give you my suggestions on what to plant in your garden, but be sure to ask your friends and family if they have any favorites.

Week Three (MID- TO LATE FEBRUARY) *Order seeds.*

For this garden you will start the eggplants, peppers, Chinese chives, and Thai basil indoors only because they are not common at garden centers. If your garden center carries the varieties listed below as transplants, you don't need to start them indoors, although starting them is easy and fun.

Order one packet each of the following seeds:

- Snow peas: Snow peas are the flat edible pod peas that don't have any peas inside when you pick them. Dwarf Grey Sugar and Oregon Sugar Pea are good selections.
- Yard-long beans, also known as asparagus beans and dow gauk: These green beans grow up to 18 inches long. The catalogs offer only one variety.
- Spring onions, also called bunching onion, scallion, or he shi ko: Evergreen Hardy Long White or Long White Tokyo are good types.
- Chinese Broccoli, also known as Chinese kale and gai lohn: This is single-stalk broccoli whose leaves and stems are slightly more bitter than the broccoli we are used to.
- Radishes: Lo Bok Chinese radish or Daikon Japanese radish. Both of these long white radishes are crisp, sweet, and good for cooking or grating raw in a salad.

- Chinese parsley: Yuen sai is a more pungent parsley than we are used to. It is called cilantro in Spanish and is the fresh green leaves of the coriander plant.
- Thai basil: Thai basil tastes like regular Italian basil, but with a hint of anise flavor. The leaves are smaller and more pointed with a purple hue to the stems. Very attractive plant.
- Chinese chives, also called garlic chives and Chinese leeks: These are similar to regular chives, but the leaves are flat and have a hint of garlic in the flavor.
- Chinese cabbage, also known as celery or napa cabbage: Choose michilli, Jade Pagoda, Springtide, or Blues.
- Shanghai bok choy: This is the dwarf, green-stemmed version of the more familiar bok choy. It has more flavor and is very easy to grow. Choose Mei Qing Choi.
- Chinese flat cabbage: This is a nonheading type of Chinese cabbage that grows in a lovely deep-green rosette shape. The leaves and stems are equally delicious. Choose tatsoi.
- Japanese eggplant: Ichiban, Taiwan Long, Elondo, and Pingtung Long are long, slender, dark-purple eggplants that are 6 to 8 inches long but only $1^1/_2$ inches thick. They are very easy to slice and have almost no seeds.
- Thai hot peppers: The Thai hot chili pepper li chaio is only 1 to 2 inches long and grows with the peppers pointing upward on the plant. Serrano is a good alternative.

Week Four (LATE FEBRUARY) *Choose garden site.*

You are going to need a garden site that is 10 feet wide and 15 feet long. Look around your backyard for a good spot that is level, is not soggy or boggy after a heavy rain, and is not in the shade. Your garden needs to receive at least six, preferably eight to ten, hours of direct sunlight to grow well. Now is a good time to trim back a bush or a branch or rearrange the backyard furniture to get the garden site just the way you want it.

Week Five (EARLY MARCH) *Start seeds indoors; buy organic matter, fertilizer, and other supplies at your garden center.*

To start your Thai pepper, Thai basil, Chinese chive, and Japanese eggplant seedlings indoors, you will need some supplies. I suggest getting a seed-starting kit that is already assembled for you or assembling your own with a mini-greenhouse, a small bag of potting soil, and twenty-four 2$^1/_4$–inch peat pots.

Plant six pots of each of four different plants. You won't plant all the seedlings in the garden, but it's a good idea to plant extra in case of accidents or failures. You can always give away or swap the extra ones.

Here's how you do it:

Fill the peat pots with soil almost to the top. Press down lightly. Sprinkle four eggplant seeds in one pot, cover with 1 teaspoon of potting soil and press down lightly. Repeat with the five other eggplant pots. Follow the same procedure for the other three packets until you have planted twenty-four pots. Sprinkle a teaspoon of water gently onto each pot, put the pots in the greenhouse, and put the lid on. Place the greenhouse in a sunny, warm location. A sunny windowsill in a warm kitchen is ideal. Water the pots every day and keep them warm. In a week or so, the seeds will sprout.

Soon you will be preparing your garden soil. Here is a shopping list of things you need to buy. Please read the chapters on tools and on soil building in Part 1 of this book.

- Tools as suggested in the chapter on tools
- Four 40-pound bags of organic matter, preferably compost or composted manure
- One 4-cubic-foot bag of sphagnum peat moss
- One 2.5- or 5-pound box of natural organic fertilizer blended for vegetable gardens. If your garden center carries only 10-pound bags, go ahead and buy one because you will use much of it this year and it will store well for next year.
- Pea fence and bean trellis. Both snow peas and yard-long beans like to grow supported on a fence or trellis. A fence or trellis is easy to build. Buy six 5-foot-long wooden or metal stakes and two 7-foot-long pieces of wire or mesh fencing that is 3 to 4 feet high.

Week Six (MID- TO LATE MARCH) *Prepare garden soil; keep indoor seedlings warm and watered.*

Preparing the soil of your garden is the most important thing you can do to guarantee its success. Mark the 10-foot by 15-foot area of your garden and clear off any grass or sod growing there. Dig the area by hand with a forked spade, making sure to break up all the clods. This is good exercise, but you might prefer to rent a rotary tiller for a day and let the machine do the work for you, or hire a lawn service with a Rototiller.

After the ground is dug up, open the bags of compost and spread the contents over the entire area of the garden. Open the bag of peat moss and spread that around, too. Following the manufacturer's instructions on the box or bag of fertilizer you bought, sprinkle the correct amount over your garden. Dig all the compost, peat moss, and fertilizer into the soil to a depth of 6 inches. Rake the soil smooth, and you are ready to plant.

Watch the seedlings that you started indoors. Make sure the pots are warm and adequately watered. The pots should be moist but not damp. Once the seedlings have sprouted, it is important to remove the greenhouse lid during the day so the seedlings don't get too hot. Replace the lid at night to keep in the warmth.

Week Seven (LATE MARCH TO EARLY APRIL) *Plant peas, onions, broccoli, radishes, and parsley.*

Snow peas, spring onions, Chinese broccoli, radishes, and parsley all like to be planted as soon as the ground can be worked so that they can grow in the cool days of spring. Please refer to the planting chart at the beginning of this chapter.

Build your pea fence along the back half of the garden by marking a row 7 feet long, 18 inches from the edge of the garden. Drive a stake into the ground at either end of that row and one in the middle. Run the fencing along the row and attach it to the stakes. Dig a 1-inch-deep trench on either side of the bottom of the fence. Plant the pea seeds 2 inches apart on either side. Cover with soil, firm the soil down, and water.

For the spring onions move forward from the pea fence 18 inches and mark a row 7 feet long. Dig a trench $1/4$ to $1/2$ inch deep and plant the onion seeds $^1/_2$ inch apart in the row. Cover with soil, firm down, and water. Mark another 7-foot-long row 12 inches away from the onions. Plant another row of onions in exactly the same way.

For the Chinese broccoli, move 18 inches away from the second onion row and mark a 7-foot row. Dig a trench $^1/_2$ inch deep and plant the seeds, spacing them 1 inch apart. Cover with soil, firm down, and water.

For the Chinese parsley move 18 inches away from the broccoli row and mark a 7-foot row. Dig a trench only 4 feet long and $^1/_2$ inch deep. The rest of this row will be planted later with chives. Plant the parsley seeds 1 inch apart in the row. Cover with soil, firm down, and water.

For the Daikon radishes, move 18 inches away from the parsley and mark a row 7 feet long. Dig a trench $^1/_2$ inch deep and plant the seeds, spacing them 2 inches apart in the row. Cover with soil, firm down, and water.

Keep your seeds watered every day, unless it rains, until they germinate in a week to ten days. You want the soil to be moist but not soggy. If any seeds don't come up, leaving bare patches in the row, simply replant those areas and keep them watered.

Week Eight (MID-APRIL) *Tend your seedlings.*

The seedlings in your greenhouse are three weeks old now, and they should be growing well. It is time to eliminate all but one plant in the pot. Find the one seedling that is both most centrally located and strongest. Remove the other seedlings by lifting them out carefully or cutting them off gently with a knife or scissors. Put the pots back in the greenhouse and let them grow some more.

Week Nine (LATE APRIL) *Keep seeds watered.*

Keeping your seeds in the garden watered until they germinate is very important. Seeds are quite fragile once they are in the soil, and they need water to sprout. Water often and pull up any weeds and clear any fallen debris like leaves or twigs.

Week Ten (EARLY TO MID-MAY) *Plant cabbages.*

The three types of Chinese cabbage you are growing in your garden this year should not be planted too early. Cabbages like to grow in cool weather (but not too cool). As long as your nighttime temperatures are consistently not dropping below 50 degrees anymore, now is a good time to plant them in the garden.

Since it has been a couple weeks since you prepared the garden soil, get out the rake and rough up the soil where you are now going to plant the three rows of Chinese cabbage. Please refer to the planting diagram.

For the tatsoi flat cabbage, mark a 7-foot-long row 18 inches from the front left edge of the garden. Dig a trench $^1/_4$ inch deep and plant the seeds 1 inch apart in the row. You will later thin the rows to let the plants stand 6 inches apart.

For the Mei Qing Choi bok choy, mark a 7-foot row 18 inches away from the tatsoi. Dig a trench $^1/_4$ inch deep, plant the seeds 1 inch apart in the row, cover with soil, firm down, and water. You will later thin the row to let the plants stand 6 inches apart.

For the Chinese cabbage mark another 7-foot row 18 inches from the bok choy. Dig a trench $^1/_4$ inch deep, plant the seeds 1 inch apart in the row, cover with soil, firm down, and water. You will thin these plants to stand 6 inches apart in the row later on.

You should have about half a packet of seeds left over for each of these three vegetables. Seal the packets carefully and save them. Later this summer you can make another planting of these cabbages if you want to enjoy a wonderful crop of fall vegetables that will last until cold weather sets in.

Week Eleven (MID- TO LATE MAY) *Pull weeds; water cabbages.*

It's been three weeks since you planted your peas, onions, broccoli, parsley, and Daikon radishes. Pull up any weeds that might be trying to grow in and between these rows. The peas should be growing up on the fence.

Keep all the cabbages you planted last week well watered to get them to sprout.

Week Twelve (LATE MAY) Plant yard-long beans.

As soon as all danger of frost has passed in your area, you can plant your yard-long beans. Please look at the garden diagram at the beginning of this chapter. To make the trellis, mark a row 7 feet long across the back of the garden, 18 inches in from the edge of the garden. Drive three stakes into the ground, one at either end of the row and one in the middle. Attach the fencing along the three stakes and secure it with wire or string.

Dig a trench 1 inch deep along the base of both sides of the fence. Plant the beans 2 inches apart in the row. Cover with soil, firm down, and water.

Week Thirteen (LATE MAY TO EARLY JUNE) *Plant peppers, eggplants, basil, and chives.*

If you started your seedlings indoors in early March, they should be ready to be transplanted in the garden now. Two or three days before you plan to plant them, place them outside in the shade to get accustomed to outdoor temperatures and conditions. This helps toughen them up.

Please refer to the garden diagram at the beginning of this chapter. Place your two pepper plants 2 feet away from the bean trellis and 2 feet apart. Place the two eggplants 2 feet away from the peppers and 2 feet apart in the row. The Thai basil plants are smaller than the others, so you can place them as a foursome at the end of the eggplant and pepper rows.

Plant all eight of these plants in the same way. Dig a hole slightly larger than the peat pot. Break up any clumps and remove any rocks. Add a teaspoon of natural organic fertilizer to the hole, place the peat pot down into the hole, gather the soil up around the stem, firm down, and water. Repeat for the peppers, eggplants, and basil.

Move over to the other side of your garden and find the half row of Chinese parsley you planted earlier. Plant the chives in the remaining row. If you were lucky, you will have six pots of chives to plant. Space them approximately 6 inches apart in the rows and plant them by digging a hole slightly larger than the peat pot. Add a teaspoon of natural organic fertilizer to the hole, place the peat pot in the hole, firm the soil up around the plants, firm down the soil, and water.

Week Fourteen (MID-JUNE) *Patrol for pests; harvest and cook Daikon.*

It is never too early to watch for insect pests in your garden. You shouldn't have any disease problems because your soil is very rich and because the vegetables you have planted are all disease-resistant. Please read the chapter on environmental pest control in Part 1 of this book.

Flea beetles will almost immediately start eating the leaves of your Chinese cabbages, bok choy, tatsoi, and eggplants. Flea beetles are tiny, black insects that hop around like fleas. They perforate the leaves of plants and can severely weaken the plants, especially eggplants. Coat the leaves with rotenone or pyrethrum powder or spray according to manufacturer's instructions.

Cabbage worms are likely to eat your Chinese cabbages, bok choy, and tatsoi. Cabbage worms are 1 1/2-inch-long pale-green worms that arch their back as they crawl along, eating holes in your cabbage leaves. If you spot them, treat with *Bacillus thuringiensis* var. 'Berliner,' also known as Dipel, according to manufacturer's instructions.

Your Daikon Japanese or Lo Bok Chinese radishes will be the first vegetables you can harvest and cook from your Asian vegetable garden. You can eat them raw, grated in a salad that is tossed with a soy sauce dressing; you can add them to a taco instead of carrots; or you can slice Daikon thinly or into sticks to serve as a vegetable on your crudité platter. Simply pull the radishes up from the ground, wash them, trim the tops, and start eating or cooking. They will store up to two weeks in the refrigerator crisper.

Week Fifteen (MID- TO LATE JUNE) *Harvest and cook peas.*

Snow peas are one of everybody's favorite dishes in Chinese restaurants. At the grocery store they are always incredibly expensive. Now you can splurge and eat as many snow peas as you like because your plants are very productive. Pick your snow peas, taking care not to tear off the tops of the vines. If the weather is cool and there is ample rain, your peas may blossom again and give you a second crop.

Snow Peas with Crispy Shrimp

1 pound snow peas

1 pound raw, medium-sized shrimp

1/2 teaspoon salt

1/8 teaspoon baking soda

1 teaspoon cornstarch

1 unbeaten egg white

1/4 cup peanut or vegetable oil

1 teaspoon rice wine or dry sherry

1/2 teaspoon soy sauce

1/4 cup chicken stock or water

1. Wash the peas and trim off the stems and ends. Reserve.

2. Shell and devein the shrimp, leaving the tails intact. Pat dry. Place shrimp in a medium mixing bowl and add the salt, baking soda, cornstarch, and egg white. Mix well.

3. Heat the oil in a wok or deep-sided skilled over high heat. Add the shrimp and stir-fry for one minute. Remove from pan and keep warm.

4. Drain off all but 1 tablespoon of oil and stir-fry the peas over medium heat for one minute. Add the wine, soy sauce, and chicken stock and cook another minute.

5. Return the shrimp to the pan and cook for one minute until the shrimp and peas are thoroughly heated. Serve immediately with rice.

Serves 4

Week Sixteen (LATE JUNE TO EARLY JULY) *Water; mulch.*

This is the time of year that the rains stop, the sun turns up the heat, and your garden can start to shrivel. You need to water it, and the best way is with a soaker hose. Simply lace a 50-foot-length of soaker hose through the garden in an S pattern. A soaker hose drenches the ground 18 inches on either side of its path, so this is all the hose you'll need.

Leave the soaker hose in the garden and simply run a regular hose from it to the spigot on the outside of your house when it is time to water. Turn on the water and let it run for two to four hours, which should be enough time to soak the ground to a depth of 6 inches. Don't water again for another week.

To retain water and control weeds, now is the time to mulch your garden. Buy three bales of straw or mulched hay at your garden center. It is better to avoid fresh hay because it will contain thousands of weed seeds. Straw has no seeds.

Simply tear the bales apart and scatter the straw around the plants and between the rows. Make the layer a good 4 inches thick. The straw will settle down and eventually decompose by springtime next year. You can place the mulch right over the soaker hose; it won't hurt it.

Week Seventeen (EARLY JULY) *Thin rows; harvest broccoli.*

You now need to thin the rows of cabbage, bok choy, and tatsoi. Simply pull up tiny plants, leaving 6 inches between the remaining plants. The thinnings will make great additions to any stir-fry or cabbage salad.

You can thin the row of Chinese broccoli by harvesting several of the larger stalks that have started to form florets at the top that resemble broccoli. Pull the entire plant from the ground; cut off the root and any tough stem. You can use the tender stem and the leaves in the following recipe.

Chinese Broccoli in Ginger and Wine Sauce

1 pound Chinese broccoli

3 tablespoons peanut oil

1 tablespoon fresh ginger, minced

3 cloves minced garlic

3 tablespoons light soy sauce

2 teaspoons brown sugar

1 teaspoon sesame oil

¼ cup dry sherry

1 teaspoon cornstarch mixed with 3 tablespoons water

1. Wash and chop the broccoli into 2-inch-long pieces.

2. Heat the peanut oil in a wok or skillet over medium-high heat. Add the broccoli and stir-fry for three to five minutes, stirring constantly. Add ginger and garlic and stir-fry for one minute.

3. In a separate bowl combine brown sugar, soy sauce, sesame oil, and wine. Pour over broccoli and cook ten seconds. Add cornstarch and water mixture and cook for fifteen seconds. Pour onto a plate and serve.

Serves 4 as part of a larger Chinese meal

Week Eighteen (MID-JULY) *Harvest cabbage.*

Your Mei Qing Choi and tatsoi cabbage should be ready to harvest now. Your larger Chinese cabbages will be ready in a week or so, although you could start eating them now. All your cabbages will retain their color and quality in the garden as long as you keep them watered. They will also store well wrapped in plastic in your refrigerator for up to a month. All three of these cabbages are interchangeable in cooking, and a little bit of each makes a great stir-fry along with beef.

Imperial Steak
with Chinese Cabbages

1 small head each bok choy and tatsoi cabbages

4 to 5 leaves Chinese cabbage

8 whole, dried Chinese mushrooms

8 ounces filet of beef or tender steak, cut in ³/₄-inch cubes

2 tablespoons safflower or peanut oil

1 tablespoon dry sherry

1 cup chicken stock

1 tablespoon prepared oyster sauce (available in Chinese groceries)

1 tablespoon cornstarch dissolved in 3 tablespoons water

1. Wash and separate bok choy and tatsoi heads. Wash Chinese cabbage leaves. Chop all the leaves into ¹/₂-inch-thick slices.

2. Place the mushrooms in a small mixing bowl and cover with warm water. Soak mushrooms for twenty minutes. Drain and slice.

3. Add 1 tablespoon oil to a wok or deep-sided skillet over medium-high heat. Stir-fry the steak for two minutes. Add the sherry and continue cooking two minutes more. Remove beef and keep warm.

4. Add the remaining oil to the wok and stir-fry the cabbages for two minutes, stirring often. Add the chicken stock; cover and cook for two minutes.

5. Add the oyster sauce and cornstarch mixture to the wok and cook for thirty seconds. Return the steak to the wok and cook one minute, stirring often. Serve immediately.

Serves 4

Week Nineteen (LATE JULY) Fertilize.

Now that you are eating your garden vegetable plants, they need a little bit of extra food, too. Feed your garden this week with more natural organic fertilizer. Add 1 to 2 tablespoons of natural organic fertilizer to the base of each pepper plant, each eggplant, and each Thai basil plant. Sprinkle a half-cup of fertilizer along each row of cabbage, broccoli, and yard-long beans. The radishes, parsley, and chives don't need additional fertilizer. Try to sprinkle the fertilizer along the soil, avoiding getting any on the leaves. If any gets on the leaves, simply wash it off with your watering can.

Grilled Chicken with Chinese Parsley

Chicken chunks marinated in Chinese parsley and other seasonings and then grilled over a charcoal fire are a popular street food in many parts of Southeast Asia.

> *2 pounds boneless chicken breast or thighs*
> *16 bamboo skewers*
> *$^1/_2$ cup Chinese parsley, chopped*
> *2 tablespoons lemon or lime juice, or a mixture*
> *2 Thai hot peppers, minced*
> *1 tablespoon fresh garlic, minced*
> *1 tablespoon sweet Thai or American chili sauce*
> *salt and pepper to taste*

1. Cut the chicken into bite-sized pieces and thread them onto the skewers. Lay them across the bottom of a cake pan.

2. Make the marinade by mixing together the parsley, lemon or lime juice, Thai peppers, garlic, chili sauce, salt, and pepper. Pour the marinade over the chicken chunks and marinate overnight in the refrigerator or one hour at room temperature.

3. Prepare a charcoal grill or heat your broiler. Cook the chicken chunks quickly, no more than five minutes total, so they don't dry out. Serve immediately as an appetizer.

Serves 4 to 6

Week Twenty (EARLY AUGUST) *Harvest beans.*

You've probably noticed that your yard-long beans are vigorous growers. The beans themselves will grow up to 18 inches long, but I think it is better to harvest them at 12 inches when they are a little more tender. You'll enjoy their beany flavor. You can cook them in any favorite recipe for green beans, or try this unusual salad, which also includes your Daikon radish.

Indonesian Green Bean Salad

1 pound yard-long beans, cut into 2-inch lengths
2 Daikon radishes, peeled and cut into 2-inch julienne strips
$1/2$ bunch watercress, tough stems removed
1 clove garlic, minced
1 Thai hot chili pepper, seeded and minced
$1/2$ teaspoon sugar
$1/2$ teaspoon salt
1 tablespoon rice wine vinegar
3 tablespoons peanut oil
$1/4$ cup dried unsweetened coconut

1. Bring 2 quarts of water to boil in a 4-quart soup pot. Add the green beans and cook for five minutes over medium heat. Add the radishes and cook for another 2 minutes. Drain and let cool.

2. Chop the watercress leaves and place them in a large bowl. Add the garlic, chili pepper, sugar, salt, vinegar, and oil. Whisk to make a creamy dressing.

3. Add the beans and radishes to the dressing and toss. Add the coconut and toss again. Allow to marinate for thirty minutes.

Serves 4

Week Twenty-one (MID-AUGUST) *Plant cabbages for fall; harvest eggplant.*

The Chinese cabbage, tatsoi, and Mei Qing Choi actually prefer to grow in the cooler days of fall. If you have the time and inclination, now is a good time to make a second planting of these wonderful vegetables.

Pull up your spent pea vines and place them in the compost pile. Dismantle your pea fence and put it away for the season. Using a forked spade, dig the soil where the pea fence was. Sprinkle the soil with $1/2$ cup of natural organic fertilizer and rake the area smooth.

Mark a 7-foot-long row and dig a trench $1/2$ inch deep. Plant three equal portions of cabbage, tatsoi, and bok choy in the rows, spacing the seeds 1 inch apart. Cover with soil, firm down, and water. Water the row every day with a watering can until the seeds sprout. (In three weeks you will thin the rows to leave 6 inches between plants.) The cabbages can take light frost and may last all the way till Thanksgiving.

You may have noticed that the eggplants you are growing stem from exotic-looking plants with lovely purple blossoms. The fruits are long, like fingers, rather than squat, like regular fat eggplant. Keep these beauties picked, and they will produce more.

Stir-Fried Eggplant with Black Bean Sauce

1 large or two medium Japanese eggplants, sliced into $1/2$-inch-thick moons

2 tablespoons black bean sauce (available in Chinese groceries)

1 teaspoon fresh ginger, minced

1 clove garlic, minced

2 tablespoons vegetable oil

2 teaspoons soy sauce

1 teaspoon dry sherry

$1/4$ cup water

1. Heat a wok or deep-sided skillet over medium heat for two minutes. Add the oil and stir-fry the eggplant slices for three minutes, stirring often.

2. In a separate bowl combine the bean sauce, ginger, garlic, soy sauce, sherry, and water. Stir. Pour over eggplant slices and cook for three minutes, stirring often. Serve immediately.

Serves 2

Week Twenty-two (LATE AUGUST) *Harvest peppers.*

Thai pepper plants are quite attractive to use as ornamentals—and they're good to eat! The fruits will turn bright red if left on the plant.

The following recipe combines Thai peppers and Thai basil in a different type of salad.

Thai Beef and Vegetable Salad with Thai Peppers and Basil

1 head Mei Qing Choi, washed and separated

5 to 6 large, green lettuce leaves

³/₄ pound rare roast beef, thinly sliced

1¹/₂ cups shredded Daikon radish

3 spring onions, trimmed and chopped

¹/₂ cup vegetable oil

1 tablespoon fish sauce

1 tablespoon soy sauce

¹/₃ cup Thai basil, minced

¹/₃ cup roasted peanuts, chopped

1. Cut the bok choy into bite-sized pieces. Place in saucepan, cover with water, and simmer for five minutes. Drain and reserve.

2. Wash and dry the lettuce leaves. Shred them and place them on individual salad plates. Layer the roast beef on the salad plates. Arrange the bok choy around the layers of beef and place a mound of shredded Daikon in the middle.

3. Make a dressing by whisking together the oil, fish sauce, and soy sauce. Sprinkle the basil leaves and peanuts over the salad and drizzle with the dressing.

Serves 4

Week Twenty-three (EARLY SEPTEMBER) *Keep up with the harvest.*

Keep picking, cooking, and eating fruits and vegetables from your Pan-Asian Garden. If you can't eat all the produce, set up a fruit stand in front of the house and let your kids sell the extra, or simply give it away.

Make a list of the items that grew well this year and any new items that you wish to plant next year.

Week Twenty-four (MID-SEPTEMBER) *Get ready for winter; nurse fall cabbages.*

It is time to start putting your garden away for the season now that cold weather is approaching.

Leave your cabbages and Daikon radishes in the garden until they are destroyed by frost. Keep eating them and enjoying them up to the end.

The garlic chives are perennials, which means that they will come up again in your garden next year all by themselves. Cover them with a handful of mulch for winter protection.

Pull up all the rest of the plants and put them in the compost pile. Cover the garden with any leftover straw or hay. When the leaves fall, rake up a few bushels and place them on the garden, too. It is better if you can shred the leaves first by putting them in a shredder or by running over them with a lawn mower.

Thin the cabbages planted in week 20 to leave 6 inches between plants and harvest them as they mature.

I hope you enjoyed your Pan-Asian Garden so much that you will plant another one next spring.

A Sunny
Cutting Garden

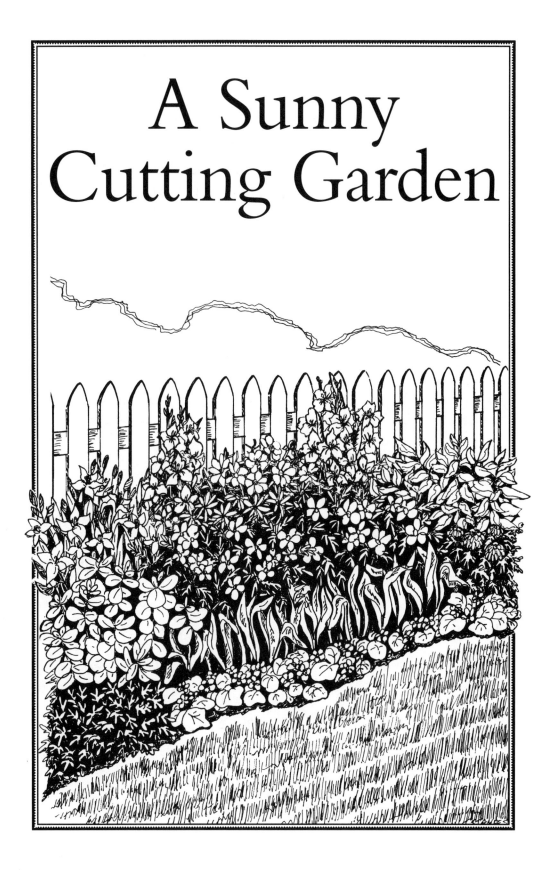

*I*magine *having your own lovely little garden that has colorful flowers in bloom from the earliest days of spring, through the warm days of summer, and on into the cooler days of fall. Think how wonderful it will be to pick these flowers at the peak of their perfection and bring them indoors for lovely bouquets and flower arrangements.*

You can have this garden with a minimum of work. It measures only 10 feet by 6 feet, and it doesn't require a lot of watering or weeding once it is established. It almost seems to grow itself. Best of all, the more you cut the flowers, the more flowers this garden will produce.

This Sunny Cutting Garden begins to bloom with daffodils and tulips in early spring, followed by peonies and irises in early summer, followed by daisies, bachelor's buttons, zinnias, asters, snapdragons, coreopsis, coral bells, and cosmos in midsummer, then gladiolus and chrysanthemums in late sum-

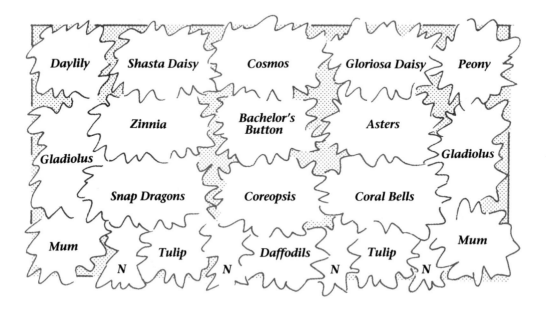

mer and early fall. Nasturtiums will be planted to produce flowers for a tiny vase. There are dozens of other bulbs, perennials, and annuals that you could grow in this garden, but these are selected because they grow on tall stems, making them perfect for picking.

This garden is so easy to grow that it doesn't warrant a weekly planting schedule. Instead I have devised a four-season schedule with tasks for each season. You will prepare the garden planting bed in the early spring months of February and March, plant it in April and May, maintain it and pick flowers from it in June, July, and August, and put it away for the winter in September or October.

The Seasonal Guide

Season One (JANUARY AND FEBRUARY) *Buy bulbs, seeds, and plants; prepare the garden site.*

Most well-stocked garden centers will have in stock all the bulbs, seeds, and bedding plants that you will need to buy for this garden. Garden centers are convenient, are good sources of information, and offer the advantage of allowing you to actually hold the plants and bulbs in your hand to judge their quality before you buy. You can also order your seeds, bulbs, and plants from catalogs. Here is a list of ones that I have used:

- Park Seed Co., Cokesbury Road, Greenwood, SC 29647. One of the best seed and plant catalogs around. Reliable seeds at good prices.
- Thompson & Morgan, P.O. Box 1308, Jackson, NJ 08527. World's largest collection of seed packets and a few bedding plants.
- W. Atlee Burpee & Co., 300 Park Avenue, Warminster, PA 18991. Wonderful selection of seeds and bedding plants at good prices.
- Wayside Gardens, One Garden Lane, Hodges, SC 29695. Incredibly huge selection of high-quality bedding plants but no seeds.
- White Flower Farm, Litchfield, CT 06759–0050. Magnificent collection of premium bedding plants but no seeds.

The catalogs of Wayside Gardens and White Flower Farm are as much like beautiful garden books as they are catalogs. Order your catalogs early in January so that you will get them by late January.

Here's what to order:

Seeds

Buy one packet each of the following:

- Asters: $1^1/_2$ to 2 feet tall with pink, white, and blue flowers
- Bachelor's buttons, also called cornflowers: $2^1/_2$ feet tall in mixed colors of blue, red, purple, and white
- Cosmos: Showy, 3- to 4-foot-tall plants. Choose either Bright Lights for red and yellow blossoms or Sensation for pink and white.
- Dwarf nasturtiums: These are 12- to 16-inch-tall plants that you will plant in the area left flowerless by the tulips and daffodils when they are finished. Nasturtiums have beautiful blossoms on short stems that are perfect in a tiny vase. Choose dwarf varieties like Alaska, Jewell, or Whirlybird, not the climbing types.
- Zinnias: Look for the multicolored $2^1/_2$- to 3-feet-tall dahlia type or giant-flowered types. Easy to grow.

Perennial Bedding Plants

Although perennials may look a little puny the first year, they grow, expand, fill out, multiply, and take up more room in your garden in the second year. Buy only one large, vigorous plant of each of these perennials, unless otherwise noted:

- Chrysanthemums: Look for two plants that are winter hardy, will grow 2 to 3 feet tall, and are classified as "decorative" mums as opposed to pompon, daisy, or spider mums. There are many lovely colors to choose from.
- Coral bells: These hardy plants have low-growing leaves that shoot up delicate pink or white flowers on 18-inch stems.
- Coreopsis: Look for the 2- to 3-feet-tall Sunray variety, which is a profuse bloomer of lovely yellow flowers that resemble daisies.
- Daylily, also known as hemerocallis: A 1-foot-tall mound of green, spiked leaves sends forth yellow, peach, or golden flowers on 2- to 3-foot-long stems.

- Gloriosa daisy, also known as rudbeckia: Large golden flowers on tall stems
- Peony: Peonies are planted in the fall, so the spring catalogs will not have them in stock. Choose a single- or double-flowered peony in either red, pink, or white.
- Shasta daisy: Large white flowers on tall stems
- Snapdragons: Buy a six-pack of snapdragon bedding plants. Make sure they are the $2^1/2$- to 3-foot-tall variety, not the 12-inch compact or dwarf variety.

Bulbs

- Gladiolus: Buy twenty-five mixed-color glads. Most catalogs and garden centers sell packets of twenty-five.
- Tulips and daffodils: Catalogs and garden centers don't start selling tulip and daffodil bulbs until late summer. Tulips and daffodils are planted in September and then come up in the garden the following spring. There are dozens of colors and shapes to choose from. Order twelve tall-stemmed tulips and twelve tall-stemmed daffodils—not the short or rock-garden varieties—in whatever colors and shapes you prefer.

Preparing the Garden Planting Bed

Depending on where you live and depending on what types of weather you are having this spring, you can start to prepare the garden site as soon as weather permits you to get outdoors and work the soil. In some of the very warm southern or Pacific coast states, you may be able to get your garden dug up as early as late January, whereas if you live in New England, you may not be able to get into your garden until late March or early April. It is good for a garden to be dug up and the soil enriched a few weeks ahead of the actual planting. As soon as weather permits, get started working the soil.

First, survey your yard to find a suitable site. This garden will measure 10 feet long and 6 feet wide. It needs to have full sun, at least six to eight hours of direct sunlight each day. A shady spot won't do. The shape is flexible, however; you can narrow it and lengthen it to fit your space, and you can even plant fewer flowers and reduce its size to fit your needs. It is best if the length of the garden runs in an east/west direction so that the taller plants in the rear will not shade the shorter plants in front. Find your garden site and mark the perimeters with stakes.

Please refer to the chapters about tools and soil in Part 1. Have ready three bushels of compost or other organic matter or three 40-pound bags of compost, organic humus, or composted manure, plus one 4-cubic-foot bag of sphagnum peat moss, plus one 2- to 5-pound box or bag of natural organic fertilizer blended for flower gardens. If your garden center carries only 10-pound bags, buy one and keep the excess sealed and stored for use next season.

Remove any grass, sod, or other plants growing in your garden area. Dig the soil to a depth of 10 inches with a forked spade or rotary tiller. You can rent a rotary tiller or have a person come rototill the garden for you.

Spread all of the compost or organic matter and peat moss over the garden. Following manufacturer's directions, spread the appropriate amount of fertilizer over the garden. Dig or till this organic matter and fertilizer into the top 6 inches of soil. Rake the garden smooth with a rake, and you are ready to plant.

Season Two (MARCH, APRIL, AND MAY) *Plant the garden.*

All your bedding plants—shasta and gloriosa daisies, daylily, chrysanthemums, coreopsis, and snapdragons—should be planted early in the spring while the weather is still cool. That would be March and early April in warmer southern states, and early April to early May in cooler northern and upper midwestern states. Ask at your garden center for the best time in your area.

In all areas you need to put these plants in the ground as soon as you get them. Choose plants that are immature and that do not have flowers on them yet, as transplants in full bloom may be past their prime.

Please refer to the garden diagram at the beginning of this chapter. It is important that you follow this diagram as closely as possible because there are three planting stages, and you need to keep track of what you planted where and when. For instance, you will not plant the peony, tulips, and daffodils until September, and you need to save a place for them.

If you can arrange it, it is preferable to transplant bedding plants on a cloudy day or in the late afternoon to avoid hammering the delicate plants with the sun's harsh rays all day long. Give all your bedding plants a thorough watering. Set the plants, still in their pots, on top of their location in the garden.

Planting Stage One: Early Spring

Plant the daylily in the back left corner. It is important to make a hole deep and wide enough to be able to spread out the roots of the lily. Dig the hole, spread the roots, and cover with soil. The crown, or point where the root meets the stem, must be kept at ground level. Firm the soil around and water.

Move to the rear side of the garden. Measure a 36-inch-long row in the middle of the back and reserve that for the cosmos. Plant the shasta daisy and the gloriosa daisy plants on either side of the soon-to-be cosmos bed. Dig a hole slightly larger and deeper than the root ball in the pot. Remove the pot and place the root ball into the hole slightly deeper than it was in the pot. Gather the soil around each plant, firm down with your hand, and water.

Move to the front of the garden and prepare to plant the coral bells, snapdragons, and coreopsis. Leave a strip 12 inches wide and 7 feet long across the front of the garden to plant the tulips and daffodils in September. Remove the snapdragons, coreopsis, and coral bells from their pots. Dig individual holes for them slightly deeper than the root balls. Place the plants down into the holes slightly deeper than they were in the pots, gather the soil around them, firm down, and water.

Now that you have the bedding plants in the ground, you can plant the seeds for the bachelor's buttons and nasturtiums.

For the bachelor's buttons draw a flat circle 2 feet long and 18 inches wide in the center of the garden between the cosmos bed and the coreopsis. Fill the circle with seeds spaced 2 inches apart, cover the seeds with $1/4$ inch of soil, firm down with your hand, and water.

 Plant the nasturtium seeds along the front strip where the tulips and daffodils will go. Simply poke them into the soil about 1 inch deep and 6 inches apart. Cover with soil and water. Next year you will poke the seeds down into the soil in and around the tulips and daffodils while they are still in bloom.

Planting Stage Two: Mid-Spring

The plants and seeds you are going to put in the garden now prefer slightly warmer weather than the earlier plants do. Plant these guys later in the spring after all danger of frost has passed: late March to early April for warmer states, May for cooler climates.

Plant the mums in the two forward corners by digging holes slightly larger than the potted root balls. Remove each plant from its pot and place it into the hole at the same depth or slightly deeper than it was in the pot. Gather the soil up around it, firm down, and water.

Plant the gladiolus by first finding their two locations on the garden diagram found at the beginning of this chapter. Mark two 3-foot-long rows and dig a trench 4 inches deep. Place half of the bulbs, better known as corms, in the trench spaced 6 inches apart. Do the same with the other row. Cover the corms with soil, firm down, and water.

Plant the cosmos along the back row of the garden. Scatter the seeds over the bed, spacing them 2 to 4 inches apart. Cover with fine soil, firm down, and water.

Plant the zinnias in their place on the left side of the garden, to the right of the gladiolus corms, behind the snapdragons, and in front of one of the daisies. Draw a flattened circle in the soil about 2 feet long and about 18 inches wide. Scatter the seeds over the area, spacing them about 2 inches apart. Cover with fine soil, firm down, and water.

Plant the asters in their place on the right side of the garden behind the coral bells and in front of the other daisy. Draw a flattened circle in the soil about 2 feet long and about 18 inches across. Scatter the aster seeds over the circle, spacing them 2 inches apart. Cover with fine soil, firm down, and water.

Use a watering can and keep everything watered so that the ground is moist but not soggy. Rain may do most of this work for you, but it is important that you keep these young plants and seeds watered until they get established.

Season Three (LATE MAY, JUNE, JULY, AUGUST) *Do light maintenance; pick flowers.*

Wrap the Daffodils and Tulips

(This task is one you won't do until next year at this time and every year after, but I want to put it here now so the garden chores are kept in sequence.)

You must leave the tulip and daffodil stems and leaves standing through the summer until they dry out and die in order to encourage good bulb growth. The stems, however, look very unsightly all summer long, so here is a way to keep them tidy looking. Gather the stems and leaves from each plant in a bunch, fold them gently over in half, and wrap them with a piece of string. This gives you room to insert your nasturtium seeds in the soil between the stems.

Water and Mulch (MAY IN THE SOUTH AND JUNE IN THE NORTH)

After the seeds have germinated and all the plants are growing well, install your irrigation system and put down a layer of mulch. Please read the chapters in Part 1 about soaker hoses and mulch.

A soaker hose is the best way to conserve water and still deliver the most effective watering system to your plants. You have already dug the soil and enriched it with organic matter. This helps the plants to send down deep roots, makes the soil more water retentive, and also makes the plants less likely to suffer from drought.

Simply snake the soaker hose through the garden in a modified S pattern. The hose will soak the ground 18 inches on either side of itself. Leave the hose in the garden for the rest of the summer. When you want to water the garden, simply attach a regular garden hose connecting the soaker with the spigot on your house. Turn the water on halfway and let the hose run for two to four hours, depending on how dry it has been in your area. Turn off the hose, disconnect the regular hose, and don't water your garden again for another week. Deep but infrequent watering makes your garden more drought-resistant.

Mulch the garden by placing a layer of mulch right over the soaker hose and around the plants. Be sure to cover all bare garden soil. Choose a mulch that appeals to your aesthetics. This is a pretty garden, so I don't think you want to use hay or straw as a mulch. Many garden centers display samples of mulches to give you an idea of what they look like. Some good mulches are compost, peat moss, shredded pine needles, or bark. Place a 2- to 4-inch layer of mulch on the garden and buy enough extra to add another layer later in the summer.

Flower-Picking Time

In your garden's second year, after the peonies, tulips, and daffodils have gotten established, the flowering order of your garden will run like this: First daffodils; then tulips; then daisies, daylilies, and coral bells; followed by snapdragons, nasturtiums, coreopsis, and bachelor's buttons; then zinnias, asters, gladiolus; and then mums. I've seen daffodils in bloom in February in the South and in April in the North, with tulips following soon after.

Pick the flowers as they come into bloom. Use a sharp knife or sharp cutting scissors and cut the stems as close to the ground as possible. This helps encourage new growth and better root development. On bushier plants like zinnia and cosmos, cut the stems as long as you can but still leave the main body of the plant intact.

Place the plants in water and shade as soon as possible. Some gardeners bring buckets of water to the cutting garden with them to place the stems in right away. Any bucket will do, but there are some attractive florists' buckets made of galvanized steel and shaped tall and thin rather than short and squat like standard buckets.

Deadheading

Deadheading is the process of removing spent flower blossoms and their stems. Dead flowers left on the plant retard the continued flowering of the plant; besides, dead flowers make your plants look tired, ragged, and uncared for. Remove all dead flowers and their stems just as if you were going to make a bouquet, but instead of putting them in a vase, toss them in the compost pile.

Season Four (SEPTEMBER AND OCTOBER) *Plant bulbs and peony; prepare for winter.*

You've just spent the lovely months of summer enjoying your sunny cutting garden. Now is the time to take care of a few things, plant your tulip and daffodil bulbs, and put your peony bush in the ground.

As soon as the first frost hits your garden, dig up your gladiolus plants with a forked spade. Brush all the dirt off them and cut the stems back to within 2 inches of the corms. Place them in a warm, dry place and let them dry out for a few weeks. Then cut off and discard any worn-out corms. Place the corms in a box or bag and place them in the basement, where they can stay cool and dry over the winter, so that you can plant them again in your garden next spring.

Daffodils and Tulips. In September dig a trench 6 inches deep, 6 inches wide, and 10 feet long between the two mums along the front edge of the garden. Spread 1 or 2 cups of high phosphorus fertilizer, such as bonemeal, in the trench and lightly scratch it into the soil. Place the daffodils in the middle and the tulips on either side, spacing the bulbs 6 inches apart. Cover with soil and firm down. The bulbs will stay in the ground over the winter and will begin to emerge in the very early spring. It is a good idea to dig up your bulbs every four or five years, separate them, and replant them for better growth.

Peony. Dig a hole 6 to 8 inches deep in the rear right corner of the garden. Work a handful of compost or peat moss into the hole and firm down lightly. Place the peony plant in the hole so that its "eyes," or little nodules, are between 1 and 2 inches below the soil level. Fill the hole with soil again, keeping the nodules at their proper depth. If a peony is planted too shallow or too deep, it will not grow well. Firm the soil with your hand.

Winter Preparation

As the cooler days and nights of autumn take hold in September and October, you need to prune back all your perennials and remove the annuals from the garden. Trim the daylily, daisies, and coreopsis to just below 6 inches tall and cover with light mulch, shredded leaves, or compost. After the mums have bloomed, prune them back to less than 6 inches tall also. Remove the asters, bachelor's buttons, cosmos, zinnias, and nasturtiums from the garden and put them in the compost bin. Cover these areas of the garden with mulch, shredded leaves, or compost.

In warmer areas where winters are not harsh, it is fine to leave your soaker hose in the garden over winter. But if freezing cold winters are the norm for you, remove your hose from the garden, clean it off, wind it up, and put it away.

If you live in an area where the ground freezes hard during the winter, it is a very good idea to place evergreen boughs over the garden soon after the ground freezes. A thick blanket of snow is just as good but unreliable. A blanket of snow or boughs helps protect the plants from harsh winter winds and temperatures and from soil upheavals caused by freezing and thawing.

You have now completed your first year of growing A Sunny Cutting Garden. Don't forget that the perennial plants in your garden will grow and expand next year, making your garden look full and lush. I hope you have enjoyed growing and picking the lovely flowers, and I hope you continue to experiment with new flowers that you find interesting and challenging to grow.

A Shady Glen

*S*hade is a wonderful thing. A canopy of shady trees around your house can keep your home nice and cool in the hot summer months and reduce your air-conditioning bill by up to 30 percent. A shady yard can provide a lovely place to set up a picnic table or a table and chairs to entertain your friends alfresco.

To many gardeners shade is a curse because they feel they can't grow flowers and that the landscape around their house looks dark and dull. A shady garden, however, can be as beautiful as any sunny flowering garden, and, believe me, it is one of the easiest gardens anyone can grow.

Let me tell you my own personal experience working with shade. The backyard of my home is very shady; only a few beams penetrate certain areas of the yard creating a wonderful dappled light. At first I wanted to cut the trees down or at least prune them severely, but my wife insisted that we keep the shade because it is so cool and really very lovely.

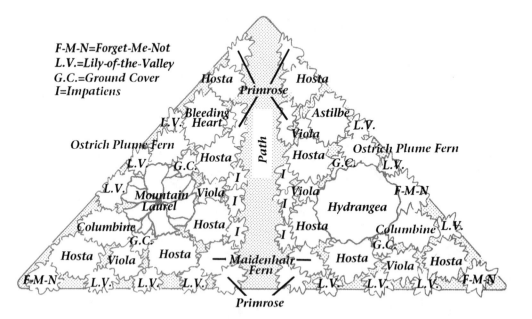

F-M-N=Forget-Me-Not
L.V.=Lily-of-the-Valley
G.C.=Ground Cover
I=Impatiens

Instead of transforming our yard into a sun bath, we decided to work with the shade and did the research necessary to find which plants grow well in shade. We worked with the natural contours of our landscape, including tree roots popping up in the middle of a favored planting site, and have discovered that we have a wonderful shady woodland glen right in our own backyard.

In this chapter I am going to translate the concept of the Shady Woodland Glen that we found hidden under our trees, and I will show you how you can do it, too. You will be planting leafy hostas, ferns, and an astilbe; romantic forget-me-nots, primroses, a bleeding heart, and lilies-of-the-valley; dainty columbines straight from the woodlands, an old fashioned hydrangea; perky impatiens and violas; a forest-floor ground cover such as woodruff, *Lamium,* or European ginger; and mountain laurel, a beautiful flowering tree that feels at home in light shade.

This garden is so easy to plant and maintain that it doesn't warrant a weekly planting schedule like some of the other gardens in this book. In fact, there are only two serious workdays necessary to create a shady glen; the rest of the year you will spend basking in its quiet beauty. I have devised a four-season schedule with tasks for each season. You will prepare the garden planting bed in the early spring months of February and March, plant it in April and May, maintain and enjoy it during June, July, and August, and prepare it for winter in September and October.

The Seasonal Guide

Season One (FEBRUARY TO MARCH) *Prepare the garden site.*

Depending on where you live and on what kinds of weather you are having this spring, you can start to prepare the garden site as soon as weather permits you to get outdoors and work the soil. In some of the very warm southern or Pacific coast states, you may be able to get your garden dug up as early as late January, but if you live in New England, you may not be able to get into your garden until late March or early April. The best garden preparation time is somewhere in between for most people. It is good for a garden to be dug up and the soil enriched a few weeks ahead of the actual planting. As soon as weather permits, get started working the soil.

Most well-stocked garden centers will carry all the ferns, plants, ground covers, and trees that you will need to buy for this garden. Garden centers are convenient and are good sources of information. In addition you can actually hold the plants and bulbs in your hand to judge their quality before you buy. You can also order your plants from catalogs, which are colorful, informative, and reliable. They usually have a greater selection than most garden centers do. Here is a list of ones that I have used:

- Shady Oaks Nursery, 700 Nineteenth Avenue, N.E., Waseca, MN 65093. Small catalog but totally devoted to shade-loving plants.
- Spring Hill, 110 West Elm Street, Tipp City, OH 45317; (309) 691–4616. Colorful catalog with shade plants at good prices.
- Wayside Gardens, One Garden Lane, Hodges, SC 29695. Incredibly huge selection of high-quality bedding plants but no seeds.
- White Flower Farm, Litchfield, CT 06759–0050. Magnificent collection of premium bedding plants but no seeds.

The catalogs of Wayside Gardens and White Flower Farm are as much like beautiful garden books as they are catalogs. Order these catalogs early in January so that you will get them by late January.

Here's what to buy at the garden center or to order from a catalog:

- Astilbe, also known as garden spirea: Astilbe is a lacy, green mound of a plant that sends up feathery flowers in pink, red, or white on long stems in either June, July, or August, depending on which variety you choose. I suggest a white flowering astilbe such as Deutschland, Queen of Holland, or Bridal Veil. Buy one plant.
- Bleeding heart (*Dicentra*): A lush-growing perennial that stands a bushy 3 feet tall and is draped with dripping pink or white flowers. Buy one plant.
- Columbine (*Aquilegia*): Delicate woodland plant with lovely flowers. Choose two with blue flowers either in a dwarf or tall variety. If you want to add a little color, choose two such as McKana's Giant.
- Ferns: Choose two tall-growing ferns such as Ostrich Plume or

Cinnamon and two low-growing ferns such as Lady Fern, Alaska, or Maidenhair fern.

- Forget-me-not (*Myosotis*): Lovely 6- to 8-inch mound of hundreds of pale blue flowers in early spring. Buy three plants.

- Ground covers: Ground covers are low-growing leafy plants, usually no more than 6 inches tall, that create leafy patches that blanket the ground. To emulate the floor of a wooded area, buy four plants of either European Ginger (*Asarum europaeum*), Sweet Woodruff (*Asperula oderata*), Beacon Silver (*Lamium maculatum*), evergreen vinca (*Vinca minor*), or English Ivy (*Hedera helix*).

- Hostas, also known as plantain lilies or shady lilies; These magnificent leafy plants (there are more than seventy different types) provide a lush, almost tropical, look to your shady glen. They are a great way to fill in your garden the first year or two while the slower-growing plants are getting under way. They do tend to spread and take over, so you can remove a few after a couple of years, find new homes for them, or just give them away. Buy eight to ten hostas that are a combination of blue-leaf, green-leaf, and variegated-leaf varieties.

- Hydrangea: Select one plant that will produce blue flowers or white flowers. Hydrangea will grow to a full 3- to 4-foot-tall plant in just three to four years.

- Impatiens: Impatiens are nice reliable plants that grow well in shade and add a colorful touch to the glen all summer long. Select one six-pack of impatiens with purple or white flowers. Try to find a pack that hasn't bloomed yet.

- Lily-of-the-Valley (*Convallaria*): Nothing is more fragrant than lilies-of-the-valley, with their tiny, white, bell-shaped flowers borne on stems above green foliage. Buy twelve "pips," which usually come in packets of six or twelve.

- Mountain laurel (*Kalmia latifolia*): Mountain laurel is a lovely 6-foot-tall evergreen shrub that is covered with pink or white blossoms in early summer. Buy one three-year-old plant.

- Primrose (*Primula*): Select six plants of giant 6-inch-tall growing primroses. Look for the rare Primula vulgaris, which is the original wild English primrose that is sometimes available.

- Viola: Select six plants of pale violet, blue, or purple violas.

Preparing Your Planting Bed

First, survey your yard to find a suitable site. Please look at the planting diagram at the beginning of this chapter. I suggest that you design and plant a shady glen in a corner of your yard that is lightly shaded. This corner will be a rough right-angled triangle separated in the middle by a narrow woodland path. The back sides will run approximately 7 feet long, and the long cross side will be approximately 15 to 18 feet long. It is difficult to be precise with the dimensions because people's yards and the extent of their shade vary so much.

The plants in this garden grow well in dappled shade, a shady area similar to that of a lightly wooded forest where occasional filtered light from sunbeams seeps through the trees. There should be plenty of light in the area, but it should be ambient light, not direct sunlight. It should be neither totally dark nor sunny.

In general you are going to plant the taller plants in the rear and the shorter ones in the front—not because the tall plants will create shade, but only so that the taller plants don't block your view of the shorter ones.

It is important that your garden site be well drained. In other words the soil can and will remain slightly damp because of the shade, but it cannot be soggy. Be sure that water from downspouts and rain drains away from your garden and doesn't form puddles.

This garden is flexible. You can narrow it and lengthen it to fit your space; you can even plant fewer flowers and reduce its size to fit your needs. Find your garden site and mark the perimeters with stakes.

Please refer to the chapters on tools and soil in Part 1 of this book. You will need a forked spade, a flat spade, a garden rake, a hand trowel, and a watering can. Have ready three bushels of homemade compost or other organic matter or three 40-pound bags of store-bought compost, organic humus, or composted manure, plus one 4-cubic-foot bag of sphagnum peat moss and one 2- to 5-pound box or bag of natural organic fertilizer blended for flower gardens. If your garden center has only 10-pound bags, buy one and keep the excess sealed and stored so that you can use it next season. You don't need a lot of fertilizer for this garden, but you do need some. You need to enrich the soil with a lot of organic matter to create the same soft, loosely textured bed that one would normally find on a woodland forest floor.

Remove any grass, sod, or other plants growing in your garden area. Dig the soil to a depth of 8 to 10 inches with a forked spade. Chances are you will not be able to use a rotary tiller in this area because you will likely have tree roots growing just below the soil surface. The important thing is that you try to dig the soil as deep as you can, working around the tree roots and trying not to damage them. Over the years you will be adding so much compost, mulch, and other organic matter to your shady glen that the soil level will rise slightly, and many of the tree roots will be left behind.

Spread all of the compost or organic matter and peat moss over the garden. Following manufacturer's directions, spread the appropriate amount of fertilizer over the garden. Dig this organic matter and fertilizer into the top 6 inches of soil. Rake the garden smooth, and you are ready to plant.

Season Two (LATE FEBRUARY TO EARLY APRIL) *Landscape the site; plant your shady woodland glen; mulch.*

The time to plant this garden is very early in the spring, after the cold winter rains and snows have given way to the slightly warmer weather of spring. Whenever the daffodils are beginning to bloom is a good time. This may be in late February in the deep South and Southwest, early March in the border states and Pacific states, and March to early April in the cooler northern states and Canada. You can plant this garden as soon as you have finished digging up the bed if you have the time.

Landscaping

Before you begin to plant, you need to landscape the area a little bit. Look at the planting diagram again. You will see that this is essentially a large triangle divided into two smaller triangles by a woodland path.

Forge your woodland path first by placing natural-looking rocks and stones on either side and then scooping 1 or 2 inches of the dirt out of the path and tossing it onto the planting beds. We lined our path with rocks that we found in a nearby stream. You may need to look around your neighborhood or garden center for the kind of rocks that appeal to you. Fill in the woodland path with shredded tree bark or tree-bark nuggets or whatever natural material you have available that suggests an authentic woodland pathway look. I used shredded tree limbs delivered from the power company's road crew. My pathway leads to a small, narrow opening between a large maple tree and the corner of my house. You might want to place a stool or piece of statuary at the end of your path. I placed another pile of rocks at the end of my downspout. You may want to make a defining structural end to your pathway or just let it wander off toward an imaginary end.

Continue to place rocks around the front edge of the garden. It isn't usually necessary to place stones at the rear side of the garden because it might be up against a foundation of a house or a fence for a backdrop.

Planting

Now you can start planting. Have your spade ready to plant the mountain laurel and hydrangea and your large hand trowel ready to set the other plants in the ground. Get your watering can ready because all your plants will need a gentle but thorough watering. After everything is planted, you need to spread a layer of mulch on top. Buy an additional 4-cubic-foot bag of sphagnum peat moss and three large 40-pound bags of shredded pine bark, cedar bark, pine needles, or your favorite mulch.

Please refer to the planting diagram at the beginning of this chapter. The mountain laurel and the hydrangea will be the two anchors for each half of the shady glen, filled in with larger ferns, astilbe, hostas, and bleeding heart. The whole glen will be sporadically edged with forget-me-nots, lilies-of-the valley, and columbines, with primroses and impatiens bordering the pathway. The ground cover will be tucked in to grow under the mountain laurel and in little nooks and crannies.

First, gather all your transplants and give them a thorough watering. Next, leave them in their pots but place them on the site in the area where they are to be planted.

Plant the mountain laurel and the hydrangea by using your spade to dig holes in the ground slightly deeper and wider than the root ball of the plant. Remove the plant from its pot and place the roots in the hole slightly deeper than they were in the pot or at the nursery. Gather the soil around the plant and firm it down and water. Mountain laurel prefers a slightly acid soil, so it is a good idea to feed it a dose of natural organic fertilizer blended for acid-loving plants each year. Hydrangea and all the other plants can be fed lightly each year with a neutral, balanced natural organic fertilizer blended for flowers. You don't need to add any additional fertilizer this year, but do feed your garden next year in the early spring by following manufacturer's instructions for the correct amount to add.

Plant the remaining plants in this order: hostas, tall ferns, astilbe, and bleeding heart. Then plant the shorter ferns, columbines, and lilies-of-the valley. Then plant the forget-me-nots, primroses, violas, and impatiens. Once all the major plants are in the ground, you can find places to make little patches of ground cover. Plant the ground cover 6 inches apart to give the plants room to grow and spread. In two or three years, you can dig up parts of your ground cover, separate the roots, and replant them in other parts of the garden.

Be sure to place the plant roots good and tight in the ground and press the soil up around them firmly. Give everything a good, thorough watering with the watering can.

Mulching

The next step is to completely mulch the ground around your newly planted shady glen. You should do this immediately after planting or within a couple of weeks if you are short on time. You don't want weeds to get a chance to get started, you want to conserve water, and you want to give your glen a finished look.

Open the bags of peat moss and shredded mulch material. I suggest that you mix equal parts of peat moss and mulch material and then layer that on the planting bed to a depth of 2 to 4 inches. Just mix the ingredients together in a tub or wheelbarrow and spread it around, making sure to get as close to your new plants as possible. Don't smother them; just cuddle them.

Season Three (June, July, and August) *Keep up light maintenance; take time to enjoy your glen.*

Ninety-nine percent of the work is done once this garden is planted. The only chores left for you to do are to water the plants once a week and add more mulch if any bare spots or weeds emerge.

A shady glen is not usually thought of as a cutting garden, but you can pick lily-of-the-valley, taller primrose, bleeding heart, hydrangea, and even viola to make colorful and interesting bouquets. The primrose, lily-of-the-valley, viola, and forget-me-not will bloom first, followed by the columbine and the bleeding heart. The hostas will grow their large canopies and perhaps bloom the first year, and the ferns will stretch out and become bushy. The blooms of the astilbe the first year will be on the small side but will burst forth next year. The mountain laurel and hydrangea will probably not bloom the first year while they are sending down roots and getting established, but they should bloom next year.

As annuals, the impatiens will bloom the first year. They are naturally self-cleaning, which means that you don't have to pull off any dead leaves because the plants shed their leaves by themselves, making room for new ones.

You see, outside an occasional watering and mulch adjustment, your shady glen demands very little work but will receive a whole lot of your attention.

Season Four (September and October) *Prepare your garden for fall.*

As the flowering plants in your shady glen finish their blooming cycle, you should remove the dead leaves and stems by cutting them off close to the plant. Place all the stems and flowers in the compost pile.

As the cold weather sets in and the garden gets hit by frost or the plants just stop blooming, you can remove the impatiens and violas from the garden and toss them in the compost pile. Violas are winter hardy in areas that have mild winters.

Prune the ferns and hostas back to 2 to 4 inches above ground level.

Place an extra blanket of compost or leftover mulch on top of the plants and around the garden. You will probably get a heavy blanket of leaves that fall on your glen because, after all, trees provided the shade. Your shady glen will benefit from a light covering of leaves 2 to 4 inches thick, but a heavy 8- to 10-inch covering could mat down and damage your plants. All these plants are very winter hardy, so you don't need to bury them with mulch for the winter, but it is good for the soil to add any additional mulch you have on hand to give the plants a little protection.

I hope you agree with me that this is the easiest garden you have ever grown. You only had to put in two days of digging and planting; the rest of your time you spent enjoying the beautiful greenery and unusual flowers. Good luck and enjoy your garden!

Appendix

Sources for Tools and Seeds

Here is an alphabetical listing of all the catalogs recommended in this book as good sources of seeds, plants, trees, shrubs, tools, and supplies. It is by no means a complete listing of all the dozens of catalogs you can get, but it is a collection of catalogs I have used or am familiar with. Most include telephone numbers, but some companies prefer not to list their numbers.

A. M. Leonard, Inc., 6665 Spiker Road, Piqua, OH 45356. Purveyors of tools and supplies to professional gardeners and landscapers, but you can buy there, too, for the same reasonable prices.

The Cook's Garden, P.O. Box 535, Londonderry, VT 05148; (802) 824–3400. This catalog specializes in lettuce and salad greens, offering over fifty of them. The owner, Shep Ogden, is a dedicated gardener, author, and writer, whose grandfather, "Big Sam," helped found the organic gardening movement over fifty years ago.

Fox Hill Farm, 444 West Michigan Avenue, Parma, MI 49269. An extensive list of herb seeds and plants.

Gardener's Supply, 128 Intervale Road, Burlington, VT 05401; (802) 863–1700. Large selection of tools, irrigation equipment, cooking supplies, and other products.

Gardens Alive! 5100 Schenley Place, Lawrenceburg, IN 47025. Highly recommended for products and information.

The Good Earth Seed Company, P.O. Box 5644, Redwood City, CA 94063; (414) 364–4494. Very good Asian seed collection, plus cookbooks, Asian sauces, and Chinese woks, cleavers, and other cooking utensils.

Gurney's Seed & Nursery Co., 110 Capital Street, Yankton, SD 57079; (605) 665–1930. "Home of Hardy Northern Grown Planting Stock" and "Helping Gardeners Grow for 126 Years" are the slogans of this complete gardening catalog.

Harmony Farm Supply, P.O. Box 460, Grafton, CA 95444; (707) 823–9125. Extensive selection of irrigation equipment and comprehensive collection of hand and power tools.

Harris Seeds, 60 Saginaw Drive, Rochester, NY 14692-2960; (716) 442–0410. Well-rounded collection of seeds, including many heirloom varieties.

Heirloom Seeds, P.O. Box 245, West Elizabeth, PA 15088-0245. Small but excellent selection of seeds at good prices.

Henry Field's Seed and Nursery Co., 415 North Burnett, Shenandoah, IA 51602; (605) 665–9391. General flower and vegetable catalog with a good selection of fruits at reasonable prices.

Herb Gathering, Inc., 5742 Kenwood, Kansas City, MO 64110. Good selection of culinary herbs.

Integrated Fertility Management, 333-B Ohme Garden Road, Wenatchee, WA 98801. From deep in the heart of apple country, this catalog specializes in orchard products.

Johnny's Selected Seeds, Foss Hill Road, Albion, ME 04910; (207) 437–4301. Well-rounded seed catalog with an excellent collection of gourmet Asian vegetable seeds and herbs. Good selection of garden supplies, too. One of the best.

J. W. Jung Seed & Nursery Co., 335 High Street, Randolph, WI 53957; (414) 326–3123. Family owned and operated since 1907. One of my favorites, it has an extensive offering of classic American seeds and plants.

Kinsman Company, River Road, Point Pleasant, PA 18950; (215) 297–5613. Very good selection of English- and American-made shovels, rakes, hand tools, and watering cans.

Langenbach, P.O. Box 453, Blairstown, NJ 07825; (800) 362–1991. Quality selection of tools, irrigation equipment, shears, and some power tools.

Meadowsweet Herb Farm, 729 Mt. Holly Road, North Shrewsbury, VT 05738. Limited but well-chosen collection of herb seeds, plus a few plants.

Miller Nurseries, West Lake Road, Canandaigua, NY 14424; (800) 836–9630. Large selection of fruits, ornamental trees, and bushes.

The Natural Gardening Company, 217 San Anselmo Avenue, San Anselmo, CA 94960; (415) 456–5060. Choice selection of good quality tools, seeds, organically grown bedding plants, and other supplies.

Nichols Garden Nursery, 1109 North Pacific Highway, Albany, OR 97321. Wonderful seed catalog full of standard, gourmet, and Asian varieties, plus herbs, flowers, and supplies, all at very good prices. Highly recommended.

Northwoods Nursery, 28696 S. Cramer Road, Molalla, OR 97038; (503) 651–3737. Informative catalog with an emphasis on fruit trees good for the climate of the Pacific Northwest and the North in general.

Park Seed Co., Cokesbury Road, Greenwood, SC 29647; (803) 223–7333. One of the all-time best flower seed catalogs with a good selection of vegetables, including Asian and gourmet.

Plants of the Southwest, 930 Baca Street, Santa Fe, NM 87501. Nice selection of desert flowers, hot chili peppers, and beans collected from Native Americans.

R. H. Shumway's, P.O. Box 1, Graniteville, SC 29829; (803) 663–9771. "Good Seeds Cheap" is the motto of this old-fashioned catalog full of heirloom and classic American seeds.

Seeds Blum, Idaho City Stage, Boise, ID 83706. A small company with a large offering of heirloom seeds.

Shady Oaks Nursery, 700 Nineteenth Avenue, N.E., Waseca, MN 65093. Small catalog but totally devoted to shade-loving plants.

Shepherd's Garden Seeds, 30 Irene Street, Torrington, CT 06790; (203) 482–3638; West Coast gardeners can call (408) 335–6910. Rene Shepherd's catalog is one of the best sources for international gourmet fruit and vegetable seeds that are chosen for their taste appeal.

Smith & Hawken, 25 Corte Madera, Mill Valley, CA 94941; (415) 383–2000. Classy garden tools, classic English wooden furniture, and clothing.

Southern Exposure Seed Exchange, P.O. Box 158, North Garden, VA 22959. One of the most extensive heirloom catalogs, full of valuable information. Many varieties are selected for Mid-Atlantic and Mid-South gardeners but most are applicable to all the United States.

Spring Hill, 110 West Elm Street, Tipp City, OH 45317; (309) 691–4616. Colorful catalog with shade- and sun-loving perennials, bulbs, shrubs, and other flowers at good prices.

Stark Bros., Box 10, Louisiana, MO 63353-0010; (800) 325–4180. Stark's has been in business since 1816. They specialize in high-quality fruit trees for the backyard orchard.

Stokes Seeds Inc., Box 548, Buffalo, NY 14240; (416) 688–4300. Good all-around catalog with a fine selection of Asian seeds.

Sunrise Enterprises, P.O. Box 330058, West Hartford, CT 06133. Good selection of Asian seeds, plus flowers, live plants, and cookbooks.

Taylor Herb Gardens, Inc., 1535 Lone Oak Road, Vista, CA 92084. A few herb seeds, but mostly a good selection of herb plants.

Thompson & Morgan Seed Co., P.O. Box 1308, Jackson, NJ 08527; (908) 363–2225. This prestigious British seed house once provided seeds for Darwin's experiments and to many of the crowned heads of Europe. The largest selection of flowers in any catalog anywhere.

Walter Nicke Co., 36 McLeod Lane, Topsfield, MA 01983; (508) 887–3388. This catalog lists over three hundred tools, including a good selection of shears and clippers.

W. Atlee Burpee & Co., 300 Park Avenue, Warminster, PA 18991. One of the most complete and easy-to-read listings of seeds and live plants, plus a good selection of garden supplies.

Wayside Gardens, One Garden Lane, Hodges, SC 29659. Incredibly huge and colorful selection of beautiful, high-quality perennial bedding plants, bulbs, and shrubs.

White Flower Farm, Litchfield, CT 06759-0050. Magnificent collection of perennials, bulbs, shrubs, vines, and more in a most beautiful catalog.

If you really want the complete listing of all the seed and garden catalogs there are, get the annual edition of National Gardening Magazine's Garden Handbook, 180 Flynn Avenue, Burlington, VT 05401; (802) 863–1308.

Selected Bibliography

These are some of the books that I found helpful, useful, and inspirational when I wrote this book. You would enjoy reading them, too.

Bremness, Lesley. *The Complete Book of Herbs.* New York: Viking Studio Books, 1988.

Carr, Anna. *Rodale's Color Handbook of Garden Insects.* Emmaus, Pa.: Rodale Press, 1979.

Creasy, Rosalind. *Cooking from the Garden.* San Francisco: Sierra Club Books, 1988.

Dahlen, Martha, and Karen Phillips. *A Popular Guide to Chinese Vegetables.* New York: Crown Publishers, 1983.

Damrosch, Barbara. *The Garden Primer.* New York: Workman Publishing Co., 1988.

Larkom, Joy. *The Salad Garden.* New York: Viking Press, 1984.

Ogden, Shepherd and Ellen. *The Cook's Garden.* Emmaus, Pa.: Rodale Press, 1989.

Proulx, Annie E. *The Fine Art of Salad Gardening.* Emmaus, Pa.: Rodale Press, 1985.

Proulx, Annie E. *The Gourmet Gardener.* New York: Fawcett Columbine, 1987.

Sombke, Laurence R. *The Environmental Gardener.* New York: MasterMedia, 1991.

Swain, Roger B. *The Practical Gardener.* New York: Little, Brown and Co., 1989.

About the Author

LAURENCE SOMBKE is the author of *The Environmental Gardener,* host of the videotape "Beautiful, Easy Lawns," and author of three cookbooks. He is a frequent speaker at botanical gardens, horticultural societies, and flower shows on the subject of environmental lawn care, composting, and gardening, and his articles have appeared in *The New York Times, Family Circle, USA TODAY, Woman's Day, Food & Wine, Yard & Garden, New York Magazine,* and many other publications. He has appeared on "The Today Show" and dozens of radio and TV programs in the United States and Canada, including CNN and CNBC. He has consulted with Thompson & Morgan Seed Co., The Toro Company, Garden Way Inc., and other gardening companies. He lives and gardens with his family in Claverack, Columbia County, New York.

Index

flower bed for, 134–35
fruit trees, 142–43
patio pots, 136
pest control, 133–34
soil preparation, 134
walkway borders, 145–46
window boxes, 136–37
Eggplant, 95, 97, 99, 108, 139, 176
   stir-fried, with black bean sauce, 183

F

Ferns, 202–3, 206, 208
Fertilization, 15–16, 23
   classic American garden, 77, 78, 85
   of cottage orchard, 159
   gourmet culinary garden, 102–3, 124
   heirloom garden, 124
   organic, 15, 23
   pan-Asian vegetable garden, 181
   salad garden, 47
Fish with herb sauce, 67
Flat cabbage, 175
Flea beetles, 176–77
   control of, 27, 177
Flower gardens. *See* Cutting garden; Shady
   glen; specific types of flowers
Forget-me-nots, 203, 206, 207
Frost, protection against late frost, 80
Fruit bearing garden. *See* Cottage orchard;
   Edible landscape garden
Fruit flies, control of, 27
Fruit trees, 142–43
   planting of, 143
   pruning trees, 151, 156–57, 160

G

Gladiolus, 191, 193–94, 195
Gloriosa daisy, 191, 192
Gourmet culinary garden
   choosing seeds for, 95
   fertilization of, 102–3
   harvesting vegetables, 101, 103–4, 105,
     106, 108

herbs for, 100–101
location of, 96
mulching of, 102
pest control, 103
planting seeds, 98–99, 100
preparation for winter, 109–10
seed catalogues for, 93–94
seed starting supplies, 96
soil preparation, 97
starting seeds, 96–97
thinning seedlings, 97
thinning vegetables, 99
transplanting seedlings, 99–100
watering of, 102, 103
Grape jam, 140–41
Grapes, 140, 152
Grapevines, 139–40, 155, 157
Green beans, 85, 86
Ground covers, 203

H

Haricots verts, 95, 103, 103–4
Harvesting vegetables, 38–39, 40
Heirloom garden
   choosing seeds, 114–16
   colonial garden, 120
   fertilization of, 124
   harvesting vegetables, 120, 122, 124–30
   location of, 116
   mulching of, 123
   pest control, 123–24
   planting seeds, 118–19, 120–21
   replanting vegetables, 119
   seed catalogues for, 114
   soil preparation, 118
   starting seedlings, 116–17
   thinning seedlings, 116–17
   thinning vegetables, 119
   transplanting seedlings, 121
   watering of, 123, 124, 128
   weeding of, 123
Herb garden
   bedding herbs for, 61–63

Onions, 34, 38, 46, 51, 77, 78
Orchard. *See* Cottage orchard
Oregano, 57, 58, 59, 72
Organic fertilizers, 15

P

Pan-Asian vegetable garden
  choosing seeds, 170–71
  fertilization of, 181
  harvesting vegetables, 176–77, 179,
    182–85
  location of, 171
  mulching of, 178
  pest control, 176–77
  planting seeds, 173–75
  preparation for winter, 185
  seed catalogues, 169–70
  soil preparation, 173
  starting seeds, 172, 174
  thinning vegetables, 179
  transplanting seedlings, 176
  watering of, 178
  weeding of, 175
Parsley, 35, 42, 46, 57, 62, 115, 119, 124
  Hamburg, with potatoes au gratin, 125
Parsnips, 115, 119, 129
  skillet-grilled, 130
Pasta primavera, 51–52
Path, edible border for, 145–46
Patio pots, 136
Peaches, 151
Pears, 151
Peas, 95, 98, 101, 115, 118
  creamed, with ham, 122–23
Peony, 191, 195, 196
Peppers, 34, 36, 38, 42, 44, 48, 51, 77,
    79–80, 90, 95, 97, 99, 139
  grilled, and eggplants, 108
Pest control
  biological pest control, 25
  botanical pest control, 26
  catalogues for products, 158
  chemical, 24

common pests and control, 26–27
cultural pest control, 25
dormant oil spray, 134, 157
environmentally safe, guidelines for,
    22–24
for classic American garden, 83–84
for cottage orchard, 157–59
for deer and rodents, 156
for edible landscape garden, 133–34
for fruit trees, 157–58
for gourmet culinary garden, 103
for heirloom garden, 123–24
for pan-Asian vegetable garden, 176–77
for salad garden, 44
insect traps, 157–58
mechanical pest control, 25
pheromone lure, 157, 158
Pheromone lure, 157, 158
pH of soil, 14
Pickles, 47
Pizza, Neapolitan, with fresh basil and
    oregano, 68–69
Planters, planting vegetables, 138–39
Plum
  Damson, pie, 144
  preserves, 163
Plum trees, 152, 156
Potpourri, herbs for, 57, 67–68, 146
Primroses, 203, 206, 207
Pruning trees, fruit trees, 151, 156–57, 160
Pumpkins, 116, 120, 128, 130
Pyrethrum, 26, 83–84, 124, 134

R

Radishes, 34, 37, 40, 41, 76, 78, 79, 88, 95,
    98, 99, 116, 118, 120, 173
Raspberries, 152–53, 154, 157, 159, 160
Raspberry flummery, 161–62
Red bugs, control of, 27
Rodents, protection from, 156
Romaine lettuce, 34, 37, 44
Rosemary, 57, 62, 68, 146
  and thyme grilled chicken, 70

Rotenone, 26, 44, 83–84, 124
Rototilling garden
  equipment for, 9
  and preparing soil, 13–14, 16

S

Sage, 57, 62, 72
Salad garden
  choosing seeds, 34–35
  end of season tasks, 53
  fertilization of, 47
  harvesting vegetables, 38–39, 40, 44, 46,
    47, 48, 49–50, 51
  herbs in, 34–35, 42, 46, 49
  location of, 35
  mulching, 40, 43–44
  pest control, 44
  planning for future garden, 52
  planting seeds, 37–38, 39
  seed catalogues for, 33
  soil preparation, 37
  starting seeds, 35–37
  thinning seedlings, 37, 38
  transplanting seedlings, 38
  watering of, 38, 40, 47
  weed control, 39
Salads
  chicken, melon, and avocado, with lime
    hazelnut dressing, 108
  early garden green, 39
  edible flower, 135–36
  Indonesian green bean, 182
  late summer, 52–53
  Mediterranean, 49
  mesclun, with fresh herbs, 65–66
  Nicoise, with haricots verts, 104–5
  potato, runner beans, and Vidalia onion,
    126
  romaine Caesar, 45
  scarlet runner bean, 141–42
  spinach, with creamy dressing, 43
  spring garden tossed, 81
  Swedish cucumber, 86

  Waldorf, with grapes, 163
Savory, 57
Scale insects, control of, 27
Scallions, 170
Scarlet runner beans, 139, 141
Seedlings
  seed starting supplies, 96
  starting of, 35–37, 59–60, 97, 116–17, 172
  thinning of, 37, 38, 63, 97, 116–17, 179
  transplanting of, 38, 64, 99–100, 121, 176
Seeds
  planting of, 37–38, 39, 60–61, 78, 80,
    98–99, 100, 118–19, 173–75
  See also Catalogues
Shady glen
  landscaping site, 205–6
  maintenance for, 207–8
  mulching of, 207
  planting guidelines, 206–7
  preparation for fall, 208
  seed catalogues for, 202–3
  soil preparation, 204–5
Shasta daisy, 191, 192, 193, 195
Shrubs, for cottage orchard, 151–53
Snapdragons, 191, 192, 193, 195
Snow peas, 170, 173, 177
  with crispy shrimp, 177–78
Soil
  aeration of, 16
  fertilization of, 15–16
  mulching, 16
  pH of, 14
  preparation of, 13–15, 37, 60, 77–78, 97,
    118, 134, 154, 173, 192, 204–5
  rototilling of, 13–14, 16
Sorrel, 62, 72
Soup
  cream of vegetable, with herbs, 138
  fresh pea, with herbs, 101–2
Spinach, 34, 37, 38, 42, 43, 50
Spring onions, 173
Squash, 116, 121, 126
  scalloped, stewed with tomatoes, 127

Squash bugs, control of, 84, 124
Strawberries, 146
Succession planting, 38
Succotash, fresh garden, 87

T

Tarragon, 57, 62, 72, 100
Thai basil, 171, 172, 176
Thai beef and vegetable salad with Thai
  peppers and basil, 184
Thai peppers, 176, 184
Thuricide, 25
Thyme, 57, 62, 72, 146
Tilling, tool for, 9
Tomatoes, 34, 36, 38, 42, 48, 51, 77, 79–80,
  87, 95, 97, 99, 103, 106, 116, 117, 121,
  123, 128, 139–40
  fried green, 88
  Mediterranean, with fresh basil, 107
  support for, 44, 102
Tomato hornworm, 44
  control of, 27, 84, 103, 124
Tools
  buying guidelines, 4
  composting tools, 8
  digging tools, 5
  hand tools, 5–6
  mail order catalogs for, 10
  planting tools, 7
  power tools, 9
  watering tools, 7–8
Trellis, 77, 79, 139–40
Tulips, 191, 193, 194, 195, 196

V

Vegetable gardens. *See* Classic American

garden; Gourmet culinary garden;
  Heirloom garden; Pan-Asian vegetable
  garden; Salad garden; specific vegetables
Vines
  training vines, 128
  trellis for, 77, 79, 139–40
Violas, 135, 203, 207

W

Watering garden, 17–18
  guidelines for, 17
  and plant disease, 23
  soaking method, 17–18, 40, 82, 102, 123,
    195
  tools for, 7–8
Watermelons, 116, 121, 129
Weed control
  classic American garden, 88
  control in salad garden, 39
  for classic American garden, 82
  heirloom garden, 123
  in herb garden, 63
  pan-Asian vegetable garden, 175
  with mulch, 23
Wild strawberry, 57, 63, 66, 72
Window boxes, for herbs, 136–37
Worms, to aerate soil, 16

Y

Yard-long beans, 170, 182

Z

Zinnias, 77, 88, 190, 194, 195
Zucchini, 76, 80, 85, 86

Gardening

From lush picture books to no-nonsense practical manuals, here is a variety of beautifully produced titles on many aspects of gardening. Each of the gardening books listed is by an expert in his or her field and will provide hours of gardening enjoyment for expert and novice gardeners. Please check your local bookstore for other fine Globe Pequot Press titles, which include:

Efficient Vegetable Gardening, $14.95

The Naturalist's Garden, $15.95

The Wildflower Meadow Book, $16.95

The National Trust Book of Wild Flower Gardening, $25.95

Garden Flower Folklore, $19.95

Wildflower Folklore, $23.95; paper, $14.95

Folklore of Trees and Shrubs, $24.95

Herbs, $19.95

Dahlias, $19.95

Rhododendrons, $19.95

Fuchsias, $19.95

Climbing Roses, $19.95

Modern Garden Roses, $19.95

Azaleas, $19.95

Auriculas, $19.95

Magnolias, $19.95

The Movable Garden, $15.95

Garden Smarts, $12.95

Simple Garden Projects, $19.95

Perennial Gardens, $17.95

To order any of these titles with MasterCard or Visa, call toll-free 1-800-243-0495; in Connecticut call 1-800-962-0973. Free shipping for orders of three or more books. Shipping charge of $3.00 per book for one or two books ordered. Connecticut residents add sales tax. Ask for your free catalog of Globe Pequot's quality books on recreation, travel, nature, gardening, cooking, crafts, and more. Prices and availability subject to change.